Coping With
Your Image

Coping With Your Image

by
Sharon Carter
and
Penny Van Dyne

THE ROSEN PUBLISHING GROUP, INC.
New York

Published in 1985 by The Rosen Publishing Group
29 East 21st Street, New York City, New York 10010

First Edition

Library of Congress Cataloging in Publication Data
Carter, Sharon.
    Coping with your image.

    Summary: Discusses the importance of personal image in society, the various components that
make it up, how one's image affects one's acceptance in society, and how to remain an individual
and still project the desired image to the people around us.
    1. Social perception—Juvenile literature. 2. Self-perception—Juvenile literature. [1. Self-
perception. 2. Social perception] I. Van Dyne, Penny. II. Title.
HM132.C365 1985   302′.12   85-2418
ISBN 0-8239-0634-5

Manufactured in the United States of America

Contents

CHAPTER I

What Do You Mean, Image?

Everyone has heard the term "image," and probably used it as well. It's one of the buzzwords of the '80s. Yet a great many people don't know exactly what it means.

The definitions range from "the way you look," to some mysterious and occult showing-through of your inner soul. Even the most common explanation, "It's the way other people see you," falls short of being really helpful.

Yet the meaning of "image" is very simple: whatever other people think you are, think you do, or think they know about you from the way you look or talk is image. Keep in mind that word "think"; as we shall see, "images" can send out a lot of totally wrong messages.

Many people, particularly people in your age group who are young and idealistic, reject that definition. You tend to say, "I don't really believe that," or "I don't think it's right to judge people like that," or "Well, I don't judge a book by its cover. I wait until I know something about a person before I make up *my* mind." That sounds good, but it's almost sure not to be true. It is simply human nature to be affected by images and to make judgments on that basis.

Do you think "image" is a modern concept, or a uniquely American one? It isn't. It goes back as far as the known history of mankind.

In the graves of the first prehistoric people who buried their dead some skeletons have objects entombed with them: weapons, jewelry, and so on. These objects, which were used or worn in the person's lifetime, marked his standing in the group—as a chief, a leader, a wise man or shaman, or perhaps the wife of one. They were status symbols, part or perhaps all of the image that established his or her rank or role in the tribe.

The body of a man found recently in a peat bog in England, and remarkably well preserved, was judged to be about 2,500 years old. His neatly trimmed mustache and manicured fingernails were still intact and showed him to have been a person of importance and perhaps high rank.

In medieval times in Europe a woman could be jailed, dunked, or otherwise humiliated if she dressed "beyond her station in life," in other words, tried to convey the wrong image. In Puritan America a woman could be charged with witchcraft if she tampered with her image by using "paint" (makeup), especially if she did so to lure a man. If these practices seem a bit chauvinistic, it was perhaps because they were passed by men, who had possibly used "image" to achieve power in the first place.

Possibly no people in history were as hung up on image as were the Victorians. They believed in it to the point that they felt a person's "goodness" or "badness" showed in his face and could be judged from that. There is a theory, which makes a great deal of sense, that they never caught their most famous criminal, Jack the Ripper, simply because he didn't *look* like a depraved homicidal monster.

Consider the Sherlock Holmes stories. Holmes really didn't need all that fabled detective ability: The good people always showed their goodness, the bad people looked like villains. In *The Hound of the Baskervilles,* a woman who had done nothing worse than defy Victorian ideals of "pure and lovely womanhood" by quarreling with her impossible father and living apart from her scoundrel husband had "some coarseness of eye, some looseness of lip" to mar her beauty.

You might still say, "Well, maybe so, but *I* don't judge people by their looks!" and you might honestly think you don't.

But let's imagine a situation and your reactions to it, or those of other people of your age.

Imagine it's the first week of school and the principal is on the platform with four people sitting in a row behind him. He is making his "Welcome back and it's going to be a great year" speech.

The first of the four people is a man. He's about five feet four and rather thin. He wears glasses, is getting a little bald, and is dressed in dark pants, a white shirt, a tie, and a knitted argyle vest. He seems rather nervous and starts slightly when anyone speaks to him.

Next is a woman, tall and with a stocky, muscular build. Her hair is streaked with gray and pulled back in a severe bun. She wears wire-rimmed glasses, no makeup, a man-tailored blazer and skirt, a hat, and what your grandmother would call "sensible" shoes.

You aren't sure whether to classify the person next to her as a "woman" or a "girl"; she doesn't look much older than you. She's short and thin with fluffy blonde hair, has on a lot of makeup very attractively applied, and is wearing a frilly pink dress and ankle-strap high heels. When someone speaks to her the people in the front rows can hear her giggle as she replies.

The young man next to her has a neat, expensive preppy-looking haircut and is wearing a three-piece suit, glasses, white shirt, tie with a university emblem, and what looks like a gold signet ring.

None of these people are in the least bit freaky; they are common types you see every day. And now the principal is introducing them.

The first woman is the new home ec. teacher.

The first man is the new football coach.

The second woman is going to teach physics, calculus, and computer mathematics.

The last young man is a special treat, the principal announces. He's the lead guitarist of the hottest rock group out, and he's going to give a little talk to the student body.

What do you think your reactions would be to these people? What do you think the reaction of your school as a whole would be?

There would almost certainly be a shocked silence, a burst of nervous giggles, and then a trailing off into silent dismay.

Aw, come on, sir, you *are* kidding—aren't you?

Football coach! All the team members have the feeling in their stomachs that you get going over the top of a roller coaster loop. This guy doesn't look as if he could coach a hopscotch competition. He doesn't look like a football coach—he looks like Don Knotts!

The lady in the suit apparently tailored out of roofing material and that hat that seems to have been designed to deflect falling masonry looks as if her idea of the perfect "home" would be Alcatraz.

The giggler in pink would have no trouble making you believe she never got past the 5s in the multiplication table.

As for the rock star—words fail you! On stage he and the band, according to your grandfather, look like what Granddad thought he'd have to down a quart of Old Overcoat to see. There is no way you'd be willing to believe that this prim twerp, who looks like a self-satisfied Harvard MBA student, knows rock music from pet rocks.

In class or on the football field, how willing do you think students would be to listen to the first three people? Many studies have shown clearly that you *wouldn't* listen to them at all. They so strongly don't *look* as if they know what they're talking about that you would simply tune them out.

Moreover, you would probably be rather angry, feeling that they were imposters, or trying to put something over on you, although you might not realize exactly why you started bristling at the sight of them.

It takes brains and ability to teach or coach, and talent to be a musician; *looks* basically have nothing whatever to do with it. But in all of these cases the people would not be generally accepted in the roles presented because of their appearance. Image would override ability.

You may know that a thriving business in the United States now is "wardrobe engineering" or "image consulting." Businesses hire these services because they realize that many of their own people aren't as effective as they could be or should be, because customers or clients react to their image rather than their ability.

But let's bring this image business to your own stage, with a true story of a girl your age.

Brenda seemed very smart and on objective tests in school got very high marks, but her overall grades were never higher than B and were usually C.

Brenda never protested. She was a quiet girl, from a poor background; her father had deserted the family years before, and her embittered mother worked as a motel maid. She drank heavily and took little interest in Brenda's school work or attempts to look nice.

The summer before Brenda began high school, her second cousin, Bentley, who was two years older than she, was killed in an automobile accident. Bentley's mother, who had always felt sorry for Brenda, gave her all of Bentley's clothes and even a piece or two of good jewelry, such as a ring with her initials, since Brenda's were the same.

Bentley had been a preppy: the real thing, a student in a private school, sent by her banker father for a summer in Europe, and so on. Her clothes were beautiful, expensive, and the essence of the "old money" look.

To live up to her new wardrobe, Brenda got a summer job and had her hair styled. She began learning to wear makeup and started an exercise program. When school started that year, most of her friends didn't even recognize her.

But the most surprising change was in her grades: They shot

up and stayed there. Rarely did she make less than A, and by the next year she was an officer in her class and in two or three school clubs.

Talking it over with her adviser, Brenda said, "I don't understand it. It was just so different than in middle school. I studied hard there, but I never got good grades. I just thought I was dumb."

She mentioned acquiring the clothes, and the adviser said, "Maybe now that you feel better about yourself, you just applied yourself more."

Brenda agreed that was probably it, and certainly it may have been part of the explanation—but only part. The counselor may not have been aware of the rest or may not have wanted to mention it for fear it would put her colleagues in a less than favorable light.

Brenda reacted positively to her new image. But so did her teachers! Before, she had been a nondescript little ragamuffin from a bad neighborhood. Nobody from there ever amounted to anything. So her teachers tended to overlook her raised hand in class and to skim over her work and fail to give it the credit it was due.

A teacher may be less impressed with image than are a lot of people, because he or she sees a student many hours a week for nine months of the year. But teachers aren't immune to it, either. A kid who looks as if he knows what he's talking about, or as if his parents are *somebody* (money does tend to imply brains) gets a positive reaction from a teacher.

And it works both ways. Studies have shown that a teacher who dresses like someone from a poor neighborhood will be almost totally ineffective in a school of affluent kids. To the students he or she doesn't look like a teacher. She looks like the maid. He looks like the checker at the supermarket. They simply tune teacher out.

One of the authors has been a high school teacher, so we speak from experience. Teachers are human, too.

The image thing is a sort of energy loop. It's like a rock band: the better the band, the more enthusiastic the audience, and the more enthusiastic the audience, the more the band puts everything they've got into a performance.

People react to our image. We respond to their reaction by becoming more of what the image says we are. It's called a "self-fulfilling prophecy." We say we are going to become a certain thing, begin to act like that, then *become* that.

Here's another surprising example of the effect of image. In a famous research project two groups of men were hired to take part in a study in which they would call and talk on the phone to a group of women. They were not told the real purpose of the study. They thought they were testing reactions to a certain product, and the information that was the key to the research was slipped in as though it were incidental.

The men in the first group were told to call a number and—in a conversation that they knew would be recorded and studied—ask questions regarding the product. Each man was told, in an off-hand way, that the woman he was calling was very nice, but awfully plain-looking, poor thing.

The men in the second group were to call the same women and discuss the product, but each was told that the woman he would call was very, very attractive.

When researchers listened to the recordings of the calls they were amazed. The men who thought they were talking to plain women were brief, businesslike, and to the point with their questions, and the women responded in the same way. The conversations were short, and no personalities showed on the part of either person.

But the second group of men, who thought they were talking to beautiful women, reacted totally differently. They changed their tone of voice and made obvious attempts to make a good impression. And the women responded exactly the same way: Their voices became softer and more feminine, and their replies were light and witty and laughing. Conversations lasted up to an hour.

Such is the power of image.

The men were totally guided by one word—plain or attractive—but it completely changed the course of the conversation and the reactions and behavior of the people involved, even though they could not even see each other.

Behavior experts are just beginning to realize the extremely strong force of "image."

What does all this mean to you?

Just this: People *are* affected by image. They make judgments based on it. They hire people, give them chances to use their brains and ability, trust them or don't trust them, react to them, often like or dislike them because of image. And they are more inclined to do so with people in your age group, simply because you are an unknown quantity to them. You aren't so likely to have a work record or established accomplishments that they can use to judge you. They have to go pretty much by what they see.

Right now that's important. You don't need us to tell you it's a tough world at the moment. Unemployment is high, business are closing, salaries are frozen or being cut.

A lot of people your age are wondering if they are ever going to be able to get a decent job, build a good career, be able to afford a nice house, have a good life, live the "American dream" with things that earlier generations could pretty much take for granted.

No generation in America in many years has faced quite as rough going.

Coping with your own image, being able to see it and change

it and use it, *will* give you an advantage; it may even be the deciding factor in getting you where you want to go in life.

Don't misunderstand us. Image won't do everything for you. Life isn't like the movie *How to Succeed in Business Without Really Trying,* in which the appearance of being a genius and a blazing success was expected to do it all. You have to produce. You have to have basic ability and you have to work. But the right image, the best image for you and what you want to achieve, can get you in the door and give you an edge and opportunities in a great many ways.

In a tough world, why not give yourself every advantage, stack the deck in your favor as much as you possibly can?

Turn all of these things into a challenge or look at it like a puzzle to be solved, a game to be won, and the prize is a whole string of gifts to the new you.

CHAPTER II

"Uh, image? What image?"

What is *your* image?

A lot of people, when asked that, look uncomfortable and may even say, "Oh, I don't know—I don't think I really have one."

Nonsense—of course you do! People in a nudist colony have image. As the study mentioned showed, disembodied voices on the telephone have images. You as a living, breathing, person most certainly have some sort of image.

But understanding what it is can be really difficult. We can't as the poem says, "see ourselves as others see us." Often the reaction of other people that is triggered by our image simply doesn't register on us as that. We think everyone is treated like that, or that we are treated a certain way because we *are* a certain way. So judging your own image can be difficult.

Other people are the mirror you have to use. To map your own image you need to study the way they react and respond to you. Sit down and write out as many examples as you can from the following list.

Don't put all the weight on the negative side, however, or give too much credibility to one individual reaction. It's unfortunate that we humans so often seem to do this (and girls and women much more than the male of the species.) Ten people can tell us something great about ourselves and we'll shrug it off, but if one person says something negative it will send us through the rest of the day under a weight of gloom.

Don't figure your image in terms of clothes. Just because you dress punk or preppy or cowboy or whatever, don't decide that other people see you that way, and also don't forget that image involves a great many things within one framework. You can be several different kinds of preppy, for instance, and the image that you show to other people has little to do with a style of clothes.

Okay, how *do* other people see you? You can write down generalizations or specific incidents or both. Both is probably better, giving a more balanced view.

• How do people react when they find out something specific about you: a sport you participate in, ability you have, your grade average, the part of town where you live? Do they often seem surprised and actively disbelieving?

• When something has gone wrong, do you often find yourself unjustly questioned about it? Or not questioned, even though perhaps you should have been?

• Has anyone ever come to a totally wrong conclusion about you? Did you find out why?

• When you start to talk about something, do other people listen? Listen for a while and then seem to be thinking of something else? Seem to tune you out right from the start, as if you couldn't possibly know what you are talking about or be very interesting? Write down the *types* of people this happens with—family, good friends, people you know only slightly, or total strangers.

• Have you ever been not accepted by a group of people, such as a clique at school, even though you wanted to be? Or have you been regarded by another group as being "one of us" even though you didn't feel you were and were not particularly comfortable with the group or anxious to join it?

• Have you gone to apply for one kind of job and found you were being considered only for something totally different—clerical instead of secretarial, for example?

• Does a certain type tend to be the main kind of person who asks you out, and does a certain type seem to be the main kind of people who seek your friendship?

• What kind of service do you get in different types of stores? Different types of restaurants? Are there places were you are uncomfortable because you feel you don't belong? What are they and why do you feel that way?

• Have you ever wanted a particular type of clothing and had a place to wear it, but didn't buy it because "It just didn't look like *me*"? Do you know why it didn't or why you were unhappy with it? John Denver looks right and natural in a suede vest and cowboy hat and jeans. George Hamilton could go to a pool party in a tuxedo and not look out of place, it's so right for him.

You have probably seen TV shows and movies in which an actor or actress looked totally wrong for the character being played. Julie Andrews has a squeaky-clean "Mary Poppins" image: In sexy, seductive roles she just looks silly. Matt Dillon's darkly brooding good looks and remote air go with roles like those in *The Outsiders*. In *Sixteen Candles* he'd have been totally out of place. (Now and then a star pulls a real surprise, though. The sexy, elegant, dynamite Cher was stunningly good in her sleazy, scruffy role in the movie *Silkwood*.)

Try to judge yourself and the way you must seem by the way other people react to you. Before long your eye will be sharper, you will become more sensitive, and it will be easier and easier to see yourself as others see you.

CHAPTER III

Your Own Special Packaging

We tend to think of "image" as being created by what we wear or how we act, so it's easy to overlook the fact that a big part of our image come from our physical makeup. We must understand that and learn to work with it before we can be a success in other ways.

Did you know you may have had one image aspect before your birth? Your name?

That doesn't always occur to people. Or we may have only the most general notion of how and why our height and weight affect the way we appear to others. For example, you may wonder why people seem to assume you have authority, are a leader among your group of friends, when you really aren't or don't particularly want to be. Chances are that they are judging you to have authority because you are taller than most of the others. Tall people are seen as authority figures. It's that simple.

Let us make clear that, in saying this body type has this image or that body type has that image, we are by no means saying that such a person really is that way. It's only that people who don't know the person judge him or her to be that way.

Here are some body and physical characteristics and the way other people tend to see those who have them.

Tall

Most of us, if asked what changes we'd make in ourselves, first say we'd like to be a little slimmer (or a lot slimmer, as the case may be). Most also wish to be a little taller. Height is a distinct advantage.

A group of college students, ready to begin practice teaching, were asked to watch several groups of high school kids in gym class, where everyone was generally disheveled looking and wearing the same type of clothes. They were to guess what social and economic background each youngster came from. Almost unanimously, they picked the taller boys and girls as being from an affluent background. This was true of everyone but blacks. In judging blacks, the students guessed that those just slightly above average height were from affluent families. Exceptionally tall blacks, one young man said, "make me think of those ghetto basketball players," and that opinion seems to have been general.

If you are tall, you are seen as more mature, as coming from a wealthier background, and as being more intelligent and having more power and authority than shorter people.

The "authority and command" image can be a mixed blessing, especially if it isn't true. If you have ever been with a group of kids who were misbehaving and an adult jumped all over you for it, the chances are overwhelming that he or she picked the tallest kid in the group to chew out. Why? That person is viewed as having some degree of control over what the others do.

Tall people may lose any advantage they have if they don't stand up straight, and unfortunately it's very easy to develop poor posture as a teenager. There are several reasons for that. Kids who suddenly shoot up taller than their classmates often feel like freaks. They are painfully aware they stand out in class pictures like a lighthouse on a Kansas prairie, and for girls that can be particularly upsetting. In the seventh and eighth grades, when the growth spurt starts for most girls, they can feel and occasionally even look like the boys' mothers. So they slump to try to hide the difference.

Wealthy parents don't put up with poor posture. They are forever after their kids to stand up straight, and they may send them to ballet school or gymnastic classes to overcome the slouch. Behind this may be both a feeling of superiority and a desire to show it, and a drive to make their youngsters as attractive as possible.

Poorer families, for the most part, don't put so much of a premium on appearance. If the kid straightens up, fine. If he doesn't, it's no big deal. So people with poor posture tend to be discounted and undervalued, and this is increasingly true moving up the economic scale.

Have you heard the term "tall and gawky"? Probably so. Tall kids are sometimes uncoordinated and clumsy, and they may seem to be more klutzy than they really are. If they stumble, it's more noticeable because it's easier to see six feet of person tripping over his own shoes than five feet of person doing it. But tall kids are often clumsy for a purely physical reason as well. When the spurt of growth starts, the bones may grow so fast that the muscles and tendons can't keep up with them. They simply don't have the muscular support and coordination to make everything work smoothly.

Being tall has advantages, but, like almost everything else in life, it also has its drawbacks.

Short

Tall girls have more problems with adjustment and image and a more negative body image, much of the time, than do tall boys. The reverse is true with short people. Short girls have an easier time than short boys.

Short children are sometimes labeled "sissy" simply because they can't keep up with their taller classmates. They are viewed as weaklings. Generally they grow out of that.

But short people—and this is particularly true of teenagers—have a harder time getting people to take them seriously. Adults tend to see them as younger than they are and less capable and responsible than they may be. A five-foot high school senior was voicing the common complaint of many when she said, "Everyone treats me like a baby. People act like they have to *protect* me! I can't get them to take me seriously. I not only have to prove myself, I have to do it over and over and over again. And every time I hear someone call me 'cute' I want to explode!"

That is why some men and boys (and occasionally girls and women) have what is called the "Napoleon complex." Because they have to keep making an effort to hold their own, to make an impression and gain credibility in the business and sometimes the social world, they become much more aggressive and forceful than their taller brothers.

Shorter people can also feel threatened by those who are taller. One of the authors had a particularly unpleasant job working for a male boss who was about five feet four. He never hired a man taller than himself, but he hired women who were much taller and then took a delight in harassing and belittling them.

Shorter people tend not to be blamed for things they do wrong quite as much as tall ones. This is probably for a combination of reasons, from "Pick on someone your own size!" to the view that tall people have more power and more responsibility for their or others' actions.

Very Thin

"Thin is in," of course, and everyone envies the person who can pig out and not inflate like a balloon. We don't mean "fashionably thin," which we all want to be, but anorexically skinny.

Very thin people, short or tall, are more often than not largely discounted and overlooked by others. They give the impression of being ill and physically weak, and it becomes difficult for others to accept them as capable or having ability.

Overweight

Overweight isn't just a single category. There are different types of overweight, and they have slightly different images. A boy is better off, even if he is overweight, if he is heavy-boned and has big shoulders and muscular arms. An overweight girl has more of an advantage if her figure is in good proportion, like the billowy ladies of Renaissance paintings, than if shaped like Tweedle-Dee or Tweedle-Dum, with everything aggregated spherically around the middle.

They have an advantage, but not a very great one, because the image of overweight is still very negative.

Do you know why?

Most people don't. They don't know why "fat" people are a turnoff; they just know that for many people they are.

We have negative feelings toward the overweight for the same reason we do toward the very skinny: They are seen as weak. We view them as being self-indulgent, lacking self-control and willpower. It's common to say, "How could anyone eat themselves into that shape?" and there is usually a note of contempt in the statement.

The reason for that feeling is rooted very deep in our primitive brain, in instinct far below the conscious level, and it is duplicated in dozens of kinds of animal behavior.

Animals that live in herds, flocks, or communities will turn on a member of the group that is weak, ill, not able to keep up. The reason isn't cruelty or a bullying instinct, but that weak animals attract predators and that endangers all the other members of the group.

For example, take a herd of range cattle in the wild. If an animal is sick or weak, very fat and unable to keep up with the others, or has a shabby, scruffy coat that is generally a sign of weakness or illness, coyotes, wolves, or panthers will mark that animal as an easy kill. Since the predator may not stop at one victim or may be part of a pack, his presence puts the herd in danger. So the weak animal is likely to be cut out and driven away or even killed, to protect the majority of the group.

We don't run overweight people off, of course. But they do have a much harder time making others recognize and respect their abilities and accomplishments and take them seriously. That is one reason fat boys and girls often play the "clown" role. They also do it for self-protection; if they laugh at themselves first, it doesn't hurt as much when someone else does it.

Blondes

Blondes may have more fun, but they also have their problems. Most of them want to scream every time they hear "dumb blonde." They've been hearing it all their lives.

People do see blondes as less smart and less capable than dark-haired people, and blondes have a harder time making people take them seriously.

"I applied to several medical schools and had three interviews. My grades were excellent, I'd done well on the entrance test, but at the interviews the people seemed to be looking right through me," said a third-year medical student of Norwegian ancestry and with naturally silver-blonde hair. "Then a woman doctor friend of the family suggested that I dye my hair brown before the next interview. I did, and I was accepted at that school. She said, 'I had the same problem until I realized they were seeing me as a blonde party animal, the out-to-have-fun-and-catch-a-doctor-husband type. When I dyed my hair dark, they took me seriously."

Boys don't have that problem quite as much as girls, but it is there to a degree. With a very few exceptions, such as Robert Redford, almost no leading men or romantic/sex symbols have been blond. "Tall, dark and handsome," Mae West said, and it seems to hold true.

Redheads

Redheads are seen as hot-tempered, or as clowns. (How many clowns hit the spotlight wearing a fright wig the color of a fire truck? A *lot!*)

People may act defensive around redheads, or become belligerent, because they "just know" an explosion of temper is coming any minute. And because aggressiveness breeds aggressiveness, a spark of temper from someone else—plus the realization that they aren't being fair and are prejudging—can ignite a redheaded temper.

Red is the rarest of all the hair colors, and it has always had a strong image impact, positive or negative. (Redheads can't very well hide in a crowd!) In medieval times, red hair was considered the mark of a witch's offspring. During the reign of Elizabeth I, a redhead, it was considered the most beautiful and desirable of hair colors. In the United States, in 1892, Lizzie Borden was tried for the ax murder of her father and stepmother. She also had red hair—and, apparently, a temper!—and in that day it was considered ugly and a great misfortune.

One of the worst things about red hair is that almost every redhead gets stuck with a nickname, "Rusty," "Carrots," "Red," "Ronald McDonald," and so on.

Bustiness

If we asked you to draw a picture of a girl and make her look as dumb as you could without ending up with a cartoon, how would you draw her? You would probably make her blonde—and you would also probably give her a Dolly Parton bustline.

While girls who are "stacked," "built" (or whatever the term is now; those are probably hopelessly out of date) have some advantages, they also have some image problems.

Busty girls are seen as dumb. In fact, someone once published a "scientific study" that he said "proved" that as the bust measurement went up, the I.Q. went down.

Busty girls can also be seen as promiscuous. And if they turn out to be neither dumb nor free and easy, people often react negatively to them, not because of anything they have done, but because of the conflict of image and reality.

A college student, analyzing his own behavior in a psychology class, said, "I saw this girl at a party and she was built like a *Playboy* centerfold. I went over and started talking to her with . . . ideas. She was a senior, majoring in aerospace engineering, and she wasn't a one-night-stand type, you could tell that right off. I said "I'll see you later" and moved away, and when one of my friends said something about her, I found myself making a really nasty remark. I felt all steamed up, as if she'd been teasing me or leading me on, giving signals and then not following up on them, and then I realized she hadn't done a *thing*. I was making a fool of myself because my mental image didn't fit her as a person, and then I was acting as if it was *her* fault. Stupid, wasn't it?"

Yes, it was. It is also rather common.

Eyeglasses

Draw a bunch of people—portrait drawings or cartoon characters. Or even Smurfs. You want to mark one as the brains of the bunch. How do you do it?

Easy. Everybody knows that! You put glasses on him or her.

Where image is concerned, glasses equal brains.

But as every kid who started young to wear glasses knows, glasses also have negative images. Glasses equal brains, but they also equal bookworm, which means dull, which often means sissy.

Glasses once were the fate worse than death for teenage boys, but that has changed somewhat, especially now that fewer girls are finding the bellowing, chest-pounding macho type attractive or interesting.

In fact, boys who are brainy, who are leaders and are ambitious may find glasses a definite plus.

What about glasses on girls? "Men don't make passes at girls who wear glasses," runs the famous old line, and while to most males a good-looking female is good-looking, glasses or no glasses, in general glasses on a girl are less positive. Women are more open about showing their brains, and more and more men and boys are not only accepting but finding they *like* the fact that we have brains to show. Still, glasses have a negative shading.

Why? It is so easy to overdo the "brainy" look. As one senior class president said of his girlfriend, "I like Kelly's having an almost 4. grade average. She's never boring, or silly; she's always interesting. She's great, in fact! But when she puts on her glasses (she usually wears contacts) she looks like a college professor. It's like she's sort of superior to me, not equal. That bothers me. It really does."

On the other hand, some people have felt their image was that of a featherbrain, with not enough ability for a particular job. Young women going into professions such as doctor or lawyer often have that problem. They look too young and sometimes too "cute" for clients or patients to take them seriously or have faith in their medical treatment or legal advice. People with a "featherweight" image may have glasses made with plain lenses to help lend authority to their professional role.

If you wear glasses and don't particularly want to, undoubtedly you have investigated contact lenses. There have been so many new developments in the field that even what an optometrist friend calls "hard lens dropouts" can usually find a type of lens they can wear.

But if you just can't handle contacts, or you do want glasses, don't despair. Go to an optometrist you can talk with about the image aspect of glasses. If the doctor just doesn't seem to be listening, or tries to hurry you in your selection of frames, go to another optometrist. You're a big boy or big girl now, and you are entitled to get what *you* want for what will spend most of your waking hours on your face.

Boys may find that aviator glasses, rather than making them look like a bookworm, give a dashing, adventurous look. Girls usually look better and less like superbrain-but-prim in whatever is the fashion right then. Granted, glasses aren't cheap, but it's worth getting them in style and the styles don't change that rapidly.

If you have ever seen reruns of Cher in her 1950s lady-in-the-laundromat character, with fright-wig hair, skin-tight leopard pants, a cracking jawful of gum, and cat's eye glasses, you know what out-of-date styles can do to the wearer.

Posture

We touched briefly on posture in the "Tall" section, but there's more to the subject. Every teenager with a posture problem is thoroughly sick and tired of being told to straighten up. It is especially annoying when, as mentioned earlier, it's a growth-spurt problem.

Poor posture adds pounds. When you want to look your best in front of a mirror, what do you do? Automatically straighten up.

But poor posture also has image impact. It says beaten, sub-missive, cowed.

Watch for it on the Saturday morning cartoons (sometimes

those can tell you a lot about image). The scheming villain often has a curved back, but most likely to be slouching is the peasant, the beaten warrior, the humble peon groveling before the tyrant.

Poor posture is the mark of a loser. It can cause much of what you try to be and what you do to be discounted. Get an exercise book or books, and work out an exercise routine for the problem. Get rid of it. It can only hurt you.

Zits

Ugh!

Did we *have* to bring that up?

Unfortunately, yes. We know it's the curse of your teen years, and one of the authors had a terrible case as a teen.

As far as image goes, it's sad but true that a bad complexion gives an underprivileged image, the idea being that affluent people get their kids to a dermatologist at the first pop-out and threaten them with everything under the sun if they don't follow the doctor's advice.

Some parents now, especially in these days of tight money, are reluctant to take a teenager to a dermatologist, saying, "It's just part of growing up; you'll grow out of it." Or, as we heard when your age, "Keep your hands off your face and stay away from chocolate and french fries and soft drinks, and you won't have the problem."

These attitudes are harmful. Growing up with a bad skin has been the cause of painful shyness and insecurity for many people.

"Oh, you'll grow out of it!" is a very insensitive attitude to take. You may grow out of skin problems, but the emotional damage they leave may be for life.

So—go to a dermatologist even if you have to mow lawns or baby-sit to pay for it yourself. Don't let anyone tell you, "There's really nothing they can do." You will probably be pleasantly surprised. As in all fields of medicine, new things are being discovered every day.

At your age we were told, "Keep your hands off your face! The worst thing you can do is 'pick' a pimple or blackhead!"

Well, that is not only patently untrue, it's harmful both physically and image-wise. Leaving a messy skin "as is" makes you look dirty, as thought you hadn't bothered to take a bath. As one employer put it, after turning down a young man with excellent qualifications but a terrible skin and blackheads all around his neck, "Maybe it was unfair of me, but I expected him to have bad breath. Not to know what deodorant was. To smell like he hadn't had a bath in a week."

Here's the way to handle infected pimples and blackheads. According to Dr. Robert Morgan, Chief of Dermatology of St. Anthony Hospital, Oklahoma City, as long as pus is present under the skin, the outbreak cannot heal and is more likely to turn into a cyst or deep abscess. So "Keep your hands off your face" makes the problem worse, not better.

Wash your hands and face thoroughly and rinse your hands with alcohol (as it you were scrubbing for surgery!). Wet a washcloth under hot water until it is as hot as you can stand it, then hold it against your face for a few minutes. Wrap your fingers in a clean, smooth cloth (not terry; it's too rough) and gently press the blackhead or zit until nothing more comes out of the pore or until a tiny spot of blood appears; then dot the area with antiseptic and move on to the next breakout. When the pressure from your fingers begins to hurt, or you leave marks, repeat the process with the washcloth.

Don't do this just before an important event; your face may look like hamburger for a while afterwards. If your fingernails are leaving marks, crescent lines in the skin, use thicker material and get your face warmer and softer with hot water.

Some doctors no longer believe that diet has much to do with how your skin looks. But not all agree. Dr. Morgan doesn't, and he puts patients on a diet limiting greasy and oily foods (so there is less oil in the system), spices and stimulants ("because they make the oil that is present more irritating to the tissue and more likely to cause an outbreak"), and sugar ("because a diet high in sugar makes infections more frequent and more severe"). "I know it cuts out the 'fun' foods," he says, "but how well a patient sticks to it depends on how important a good skin is."

Your Name

Does it surprise you that your name is part of your image? Your name is not only *part* of your image, some behavior-study experts think it may be the single most important factor in shaping the way your personality develops.

Margaret Mitchell was a master of the art of giving people names that perfectly matched their image and character. In her great novel *Gone with the Wind*, Scarlett was vivid, vital, colorful as her name. Rhett Butler was abrupt, macho, commanding—just as the name sounds. Suellen sounds like "sullen," and Scarlett's bratty sister was sulky, spoiled, and demanding. Ashley Wilkes was indecisive, unsuccessful, and wishy-washy, not the dashing hero Scarlett considered him to be.

How can your name affect the way your own personality forms? Let us suppose three little girls, aged about eight, come flying into the house with a slam of the door, typical behavior for eight-year-olds. And let's suppose someone, say an aunt, speaks to all three of them.

"Billie Jean, don't slam the door like that." Aunt's tone is only faintly annoyed. Billie Jean is a boyish name with a tomboy image, and somehow everyone expects her to be rowdy and slam doors.

"Susan, how many times have I told you not to do that?"

The tone is sharper now. From Susan it isn't expected or permitted behavior.

"Beth!" The tone is now as shocked as if the kid had started swearing in church. The child gets the embarrassed feeling that she has done something shameful as well as totally unacceptable. Much more than Billie Jean or Susan, she is likely to be upset at the reprimand because to her it is more demeaning. As Aunt overreacts, Beth overreacts and becomes even more shy and timid and afraid of doing the wrong thing.

Have you ever known a girl with a boy's name who wasn't a tomboy? Known a girl named Beth or Dawn or April who wasn't feminine, quiet, and rather shy? You may have: The rule isn't absolute, of course. But it is true more often than not, and when the person and the name are direct opposites, that person usually goes by a nickname.

Think of the mental picture names give you. Margaret and Elizabeth sound dignified, restrained, and rather old-fashioned. Their image is "good grades, conservative clothes, favorite place—the library." It's much easier to see the head cheerleader as having a name like Susan or Kelly or Julie.

For the most part, boys' names have less strong images, and they also are less likely to go in or out of fashion. You can usually make a pretty accurate guess at a woman's age by her name, but it's harder to do with a man. The trend now is toward macho one-syllable names, such as Brad, Scott, or Kent. Names that could be either male or female, such as Carroll, Marion, Lois, or Evelyn, are not likely to be given to boys these days. In fact, you may be surprised to learn that they ever were, but at one time they were rather common.

Contrived names or those made from running two names together tend to have a somewhat second-rate image, and so do "cute" names or names in which a *y* on the end has been replaced with an *i*; for example, Terri or Luci. First names that might be last names have a more affluent effect: Courtney, Riley, Kyle, Hunter.

A Midwestern couple whose last name was Monk christened their son Chip. David Bowie named his son Zowie. Another couple, whose last name was Daub, stuck their poor innocent offspring with Zip-a-Dee-Do. One would find it hard to blame any of those kids if they burned the house down as soon as they were old enough.

Many studies have shown children with bizarre names to be handicapped. They are much more likely than the Susans, Marys, Bills, and Johns in their class to develop neurotic and often destructive and antisocial behavior. They are branded as freaks by their names, right from the start, and are most likely to be treated as freaks, react as freaks, *become* freaks. The self-fulfilling prophecy again.

A corporate executive in the Southwest admits that the dumbest thing he and his wife ever did was to name their daughter Stormi. "She spent the first fourteen years of her life acting as if she had to live up to that name," he says, with a sigh. Finally, when she was fifteen and facing the real possibility of reform school if she didn't straighten up, her parents followed the suggestion of a psychologist: They enrolled her in a rather strict private school and on every record changed her name to Anne, her middle name.

Stormi objected wildly, but to no avail. She became "Anne," and, at first sullenly and grudgingly, but finally more naturally, she began to go by the middle name. Today, two years later, she makes good grades and is over the worst of her problems.

According to the psychologist, "With a name like that, people expected her to be a little hellion, and when she wasn't, they acted disappointed. She had been programmed to be a problem from the beginning, by that name."

If names can be hard to cope with, image-wise, nicknames can be worse. How often do you find someone who goes by a nickname who doesn't hate it? Not very often. Being called

"Shorty" when you have to stoop to get through the average doorway is not only a put-down, it's witless. It just plain sounds *dumb*.

Of course, not all nicknames are dumb or a put-down. The nephew of one of the authors was proud of being tagged "Rocky" after, as a sophomore, he flattened a senior noted as a bully.

It would seem that getting rid of a name or nickname you don't like, or that hurts your image, would be fairly easy. But there's a hook about names, a psychological factor that can make it a trickier problem than it seems.

To name something gives the namer a claim, an "ownership" of the person, animal, or whatever. Many a person has gone through life with a nickname bestowed by an older brother or sister when the baby was first brought home. Being the one to name the baby helped ease the jealousy and resentment of the invader; it gave the name a special place in that person's life, and so the tag stuck.

So dumping an unwanted nickname or, worse yet, changing your real name, is likely to leave someone with hurt feelings and a sense of rejection.

You get rid of a nickname you don't like by refusing to respond to it. If someone says, "Hey, Tubby!" or "Come here a second, half-pint," you just keep going as if it meant someone else. At the second or third call you might respond with a surprised look and say, very coolly, "I didn't realize you were talking to me. My name is Rick."

Don't make a grand announcement that you are no longer going by "Red" or "Wildman" or whatever, and don't get mad when someone calls you by that name. If people discover they can get a rise out of you by use of the nickname, it will make the problem that much worse.

But what if your own name is one you can't stand, or that hurts your image?

Almost nobody likes his or her name as a youngster. Nearly everyone would have picked something else, given a choice. But there is a difference between a name that you don't care for and one that really hurts your image: Cuthwell, for example, or Hepzibah Henrietta. Or a last name like Rape, Mold, Pugh.

Unfortunately, hurtful first names, like last names, are usually family heirlooms, and trying to change can cause a real snarl of resistance and hurt family feelings.

You might choose to go by your middle name; or a shortened version of your name. Bert instead of Cuthbert, perhaps. Reta might suit you better than Henrietta.

You can also change your name legally. Once again, that is almost sure to hurt feelings, and you might wait until you are out on your own to do it. But it can be to your advantage, even if your name isn't terribly uncommon or bizarre or ugly. Richard Nixon and Charles Manson, for example, aren't terrible names, but the past record of two other people with those names can leave a lasting negative imprint on anyone else with the same name.

In thinking about changing a name, consider job applications, applications for admission to college, letters, and phone calls you make on the job. In such cases your name may be the only thing someone has to gain an image of you.

Consider whether the image helps or hurts.

CHAPTER IV

Is There One "Best" Image?

People always expect the answer to that question to be: No, there isn't; different images work best for different people. That is partly true, but only partly. Basically, yes, there is one "best" image.

We assume you are interested in your image, coping with it and perhaps changing it, because you are interested in making the most of your life: doing well in school, getting into the college you want, getting the job you want, and advancing in the career you choose.

For all of these purposes, the best image you can adopt is basically a well-to-do one. True or not (it is in some cases and most certainly isn't in others), and fair or not (no, it isn't fair, but's it's the way things are and we have to live with it), the moderately rich are regarded as being smarter, more capable, more attractive, more dependable, more ambitious than we who are "average."

Television sends us some very conflicting signals in this area, and it may be part of the reason people are inclined to doubt the truth of the situation. Because the message we get from television is exactly opposite the way life really is.

On TV, the working class people are the ones who have it all together; they are cool and smart, have fun out of life, have their heads on straight. Think about it. Fonzie, the high school dropout of "Happy Days," had the upper hand in nearly all situations and strings of girls fluttering around him. "Cheers," "Taxi," "One Day at a Time," all give the "This is the way to be!" message. *Flashdance* sparked a brief but strong fad, a whole new way to dress in cut-up sweats. The girl definitely represented a blue-collar worker. The music was great, and it left a terrific impression.

On the other hand, think of the way the affluent class is portrayed. On "Dallas," "Dynasty," "Falcon Crest," not only is everyone wretched and constantly deep in compound misery, but most of them act as if their elevators don't quite go to the top floor. *Nobody* would want to be like that, money or no money.

But in real life, a well-to-do image will get you much farther than if you give off vibes saying, "I came from the wrong side of the tracks—wanna make something of it?"

Within that "well-to-do" definition are a lot of images, however, so don't see yourself as being confined to a preppy image or a certain failure.

The well-to-do image varies in different regions of the country, and it can also vary in different career fields. It's not uncommon to see wealthy people in jeans, but their jeans won't be faded and wrinkled—they'll be pressed and have a sharp crease.

Picture a man or woman in jeans, a Western-cut suede blazer, a piece or two of real Indian jewelry, boots, and a hat. Can you image a banker in such an outfit? Nobody in the world would take him seriously—in Boston. But in the Southwest a banker may very well dress just that way; in Oklahoma or Texas it's very much an affluent look.

Does the mere idea of trying to upgrade your image make you uncomfortable? We've all known people who tried that, and often they looked phony, social-climbing, or downright silly. Others laughed at them behind their backs. Nobody wants to be in that situation. Yet you *can* improve your image, go for the best image, without making yourself look silly.

Rule number one: Don't tell anybody, unless it's a trusted friend, perhaps, what you are doing. It's natural to want to talk it over, but it's also not a good idea. Families in particular can be a problem, because they may not take what you want to do seriously, or in the right way. "Well, aren't we good enough for you, Miss La De Da? We came from plain working people and we're not ashamed of it." Can't you just hear it? We are not by any means trying to say you should be ashamed of your family, background, or origins, or should ever lie about them. We are saying that for your own good you can upgrade your image, and if you do you won't ever say, "I live on Cadillac Hill and my father's a company's president" if that isn't true. Remember, image is what people think they know about you, and if your image is topflight, few people will even question it.

CHAPTER V

Being Yourself and
Wanting to Look Like Everyone Else

When we started this book someone said, "Why bother? All teenagers just want to dress like everybody else anyway."

In a way that's not true, and in another way it's not only true but a perfect illustration of the whole idea of "image."

It's not totally true that all teens try to dress exactly alike. There are probably a number of different images in your school: punk, preppy, jock, cowboy. (Cowboy as a "look," a fad, is pretty much out now, but it still exists in a lot of schools, not because it's the fashion but because in farm and ranch areas "the look" has been the height of style for 150 years!)

Teens don't want to look like *everybody* else; they want to look like everybody else *in their chosen group*. Doing this gives you your first real experience at shaping an image for yourself. If you want to be part of the preppy bunch, you go for a preppy look yourself: polo oxford shirts, khaki slacks, pearl necklace for all occasions, Beene moccasins. You pay attention to what goes with the image and what doesn't, and you also know how preppies react when someone whose image is definitely punk tries to fit in with your crowd. (And vice versa.) In fact, looking around the average middle or high school isn't a bad way to grasp the power of image and what the image you want can do for you.

What about the old admonition, "Just be yourself; be natural"?

Working for the image you want doesn't clash with that

teaching at all. In fact, it enhances it. As we have said before, image isn't—or to work certainly shouldn't be—phony. The right image enhances "yourself." It *is* natural. You are saying, "I am basically this kind of person. I am working to be *more* of what you see. I am putting on a packaging that shows the real me."

Working on the image you want *is* being yourself.

It's funny, anyway, that "Be yourself, be natural." In the 1960s and early 1970s young people were urged by their peers, "Be yourself. Be natural. Reject conformity. Tell the Establishment to go to blazes. Let your own inner beauty shine through, man."

And what did that really mean? "Be yourself, be natural" actually meant "Be like *us*." "Reject conformity" meant reject conformity to "them," but do conform to "us" because we won't accept you in the group if you don't. It didn't matter how much "inner beauty" you had or whether or not it did shine through, but if it was trying to shine through a three-piece suit and a Brooks Brothers shirt, you were about as welcome at a gathering of the hip and rebellious as a skunk at a garden party.

So don't worry about looking like everybody else, and don't worry about yourself and being natural. Decide on the image you want and feel is right for you, work on it, and it's almost impossible that it will be phony or that you'll end up in a phony setting or not "being yourself."

CHAPTER VI

The Parts of Your Packaging It's (More or Less) Easy to Change

As members of the "flower child" generation, we understand very well that image can be a touchy area with teens. It's easy for you to resent any efforts to get you to go along with "us," the older generation. You want to look like "you," not like "them." You want to be yourselves, not clones of someone else or some other generation, no matter how wild and rebellious that generation was and how absolutely awful its parents considered it to be. You want to stake out your own place in time, and if it takes gluing your hair in points like the antenna of an old-fashioned TV set and dyeing it bright pink, some of you will do it. If you want to paint your face bright orange and screaming green we don't even really object. You, after all, are the one who is going to have to live with the consequences of pink hair and a screaming green face. (Awww, durn! The fact that your parents take a relatively cool view of the whole punk thing and aren't having 106 fits has probably taken half the fun out of it. Those of us who were hippies and beatniks remember our parents getting on their hind legs about how we dressed and looked, and how silly it all was, really.)

Just don't make one big, ridiculous error that our generation did. Some of us had jeans so thin and ragged they were practically transparent, sandals, yards of sometimes mangy-looking hair, beads, and sheepskin vests occasionally on bodies that hadn't had close contact with soap in a month or more. (Ugh! That far out we never were.) Black young people did their hair up in Afros that looked like what might happen if you set off a stick of dynamite in a Brillo pad and adopted African outfits that would do credit to a tribal chief.

We then demanded to be treated "like everybody else! After all, we're human, too." (Plenty of the older generation argued with us on that point!)

And were we treated "like everybody else"? Of course not! For the very simple reason that we *weren't* like "everybody else." Hippie dressing was a statement of rebellion, a drawing of battle lines.

Punk is a statement of rebellion, too. Just don't, as too many of our generation did, act like spoiled brats when someone expects you to live with the consequences of your choice.

An odd aspect of the hippie movement, which seems to be repeating itself in punk, is that the kids quickest to adopt both were the very rich and the poor. The rich kids knew that no matter how wild they were, they always had daddy's bucks to fall back on, and the poor felt they didn't have much to lose anyway.

The great middle class tended not to go so far overboard. We took a look at things, saw a lot we didn't like and wanted to protest, but also knew we were going to have to make our own way and get by on our own efforts in a rough world. We may have adopted the manners and dress of the hip generation and made fitting gestures, but we rarely went too far out on the proverbial limb.

That wasn't being "sheep," as the hippie put-down of the times went. It was being both more realistic and more mature about our situation than some of the bearded orators shouting on the street corners.

It's a point you need to keep in mind: Be good to yourself, be aware of your future and what it will take to make it.

Off our own personal soapbox and back to practical matters, and the image elements you can change fairly easily.

Pay attention to TV here: It's a perfect example of a lot of the points we hope to make.

• A young woman is shown getting ready to go out, with a glittery dress, a fancy hairdo, excellent makeup. She might be a model, but she isn't. She's a hooker.

• A young woman who as a high school student was a carhop in a sleazy drive-in has managed to connive her way, with lies about pregnancy, into marrying the son of a wealthy family. She's shown in a room out of a decorator's magazine, dressed in a fur-trimmed velvet robe, but basically she's a mean-spirited, lying, sneaky little witch.

• In an episode of "Hart to Hart" a young man, a former school friend of Jennifer's, is about to meet her again, and he has designs on her bod and possibly her life. He's a creep. He drives a Mercedes, wears a gold watch and expensive clothes, but he's still a grungy, low-life creep.

How do the directors of those TV shows reveal their characters' true colors?

Easily. In every case, they stick a wad of gum in the character's mouth.

Watch for that, the next time you sit down for an evening of TV. You never see a hero or heroine, a sympathetic character, someone you'd want to cheer for, chewing gum (except in the commercials, of course). When characters do chew gum, it is part of a negative image and is occasionally a hint that, although they look like good people now, before the end of the show they will be unmasked as creeps.

Most teens—at least when we were your age—think chewing gum is kinda neat: It annoys your parents, gets on your teachers' nerves, and goes along with the built-in ugliness of punk.

But it does more: It brands you instant second rate. Have you ever seen a celebrity endorsing chewing gum? No? It's probably for the simple reason that none of them wants the image that goes with it.

We know of many personnel managers who automatically reject anyone who comes to a job interview chomping away.

Get rid of the gum. You can have top grades from an exclusive private school, be dressed from the most expensive store in town, and drive to an interview in your own Porsche; all of that will count for nothing if you walk in with your jaw working away like a cow chewing its cud.

Our next point may sound as if we are on a religious-health kick. We aren't, we promise. As we have said, we are dealing with image only. You can easily verify it all for yourself.

Do you smoke? If so, why did you start? Why do most teens start? The answer generally is, "Well, I wanted to look older and more sophisticated."

Was that your reason?

Like chewing gum, smoking, especially by people your age, is used on TV to illustrate negative character. The double standard still exists, and boys may smoke and not look *too* bad; but when the director puts a cigarette in a girl's mouth you can be as sure she is No Good as your Victorian great-great-grandmother would have been.

As for looking grown up and sophisticated, hunt up kids a year or two younger than you, in an area where they are likely to be smoking. Watch them light up. Do they suddenly look your age? Do they suddenly seem more knowledgeable and worldly, more like kids you'd go out of your way to try to get to know?

Of course not. Like a little girl wearing her mother's high heels, lighting a cigarette only emphasizes what little kids they really are. They look pathetic and silly and as if no one cared enough about them to try to stop them.

The TV show "Dynasty" is a perfect example. Everybody's sweetheart, Krystal, never touches a cigarette. Villainess Alexis is rarely without one; it underlines the fact that basically she's a creep.

And as for "smokeless tobacco"—excuse us while we gag.

Smoking is the bottom of the barrel. Smokeless tobacco is picking up the barrel and crawling under it. All the ads stress the "macho—are you *man* enough for it?" approach, and for that reason a lot of guys your age try it. Maybe you impress each other. But a bulging cheek, a mouth that looks as if you've been rooting with the pigs, and spit-out black blobs makes most people faintly ill.

Listen to the manager of a big Western facility that sells race horses, where teens are often hired part time during sales. "Use smokeless tobacco now and then myself, but I'd never consider hiring anyone who showed up chewing it. It grosses out too may people. Even if you use it yourself, you don't usually want to see other people using it. When a customer is here to pay me half a million dollars for a horse, I won't take a chance of turning them off. People are warned beforehand, and I've fired a couple on the spot for forgetting."

Enough said?

CHAPTER VII

Every Time You Open Your Mouth. . .

Have you ever seen the movie *My Fair Lady?* In it one Englishman bets another that, by teaching a guttersnipe flowergirl to speak properly, he can turn her into a lady accepted in the highest society.

It makes a good story; it also has a lot of truth in it. How you sound and how you speak have a great deal to do with your image and can enormously help, or hinder, you in getting where you want to be in life.

Do you have any idea what you sound like? Probably not. Most of us think we don't have an accent and that our voice is pleasant. That being so, hearing a candid tape recording can be a real jolt. However, it can also be very good medicine for your vocal image.

Get such a recording of yourself by agreeing with friends to take turns making a tape of a group of you talking together. Trade off doing this so that only one person in the group knows the recorder is on. (No fair using it for blackmail!)

In private, listen to the recording. Play it over several times. How do you *really* sound? At all like you thought? Probably not. Few of us do.

Maybe the voice isn't an accurate reproduction; ask friends about that. But it does reproduce things like a very nasal sound, the twang that screams "hick" even though you live in New York City; and a whine, just about the most irritating sound a human voice can produce. Once you have zeroed in on the noticeable defects, you can start to change them.

Of all areas of changing, changing the way you speak and

the way you sound is probably the hardest. Why? Because talking is one of the most effortless things we do. We may start a conversation swearing inwardly to watch the way we talk, the words or phrases we use, but as we get wrapped up in what we are saying we tend to slip back into the old familiar pattern.

Trying taping a note inside your locker door, or inside a notebook cover, to remind yourself to speak more carefully, to use meaningful words, to eliminate "uh. . .uh, you know. . ." from your vocabulary.

Once again, it may not be a good idea to tell anyone you are trying to do this; you may never hear the end of it from friends or, even more likely, from family. You may have to make a particular effort to stay on the new track at home, since family members tend to talk very much alike, sometimes to the point that telephone callers can't tell who is speaking.

Changing the way your voice sounds can help improve your image, but you can make an even more notable change with words.

One of the authors recently came across an "advice for teen-agers" pamphlet printed about twenty-five years ago that stressed, "Remove all slang from your speech."

How silly can you get? Slang is one of the things that give your speech liveliness and personality. Every country and every period of history has had its own minilanguage, the slang of that time and place. By no means should you try to eliminate it.

But some expressions downgrade your image and the effect you have on others. The first that you need to make a major effort to comb out are "Yeah" and "Huh?" (Foreigners make fun of Americans for "Huh?" Of course, they have expressions equally overused.) Both of these are very second-rate, and a conversation peppered with them has been known to turn off a prospective employer or a present boss. They make you sound not particularly bright.

How do you make yourself stop using expressions you want to get rid of? A behavioral psychologist suggests this: Every time you catch yourself saying something you want to get rid of, bite the inside of your lip, hard enough to hurt but not hard enough, of course, to draw blood or be terribly painful. Or put a rubber band loosely around a wrist and give yourself a snap with it. This is called "aversion therapy," and it is surprisingly effective.

Go back to the recording of your speech. Do you sprinkle "you know" through your conversation as thickly as salt on french fries? So many people do, and that particular inane phrase, endlessly repeated, can make listeners want to stuff a boot in the speaker's mouth. Think of people (althetes seem the worst) who are interviewed on TV, and every third and fourth word is "you know." You'd think they'd been playing too much without a helmet. They sound like dolts, and it's painfully obvious to viewers. Yet a high percentage of these viewers do exactly the same thing.

Other idiotic and over-used phrases: "Know what I mean" and "like." "Like, he has this new Trans-Am and, like, it's blue and gold." Gets on your nerves very quickly.

And then there's "goes." "He goes 'Do you want to see this movie or not?' and I go 'Not if you are going to act that way about it!'" Sound familiar? This particular usage leaves a negative impression on listeners.

There's a long list of overworked words, and they seem to go in and out of fashion: "neat," "fabulous," "a no-no."

What about X-rated language?

As we said, there are fashions in words just as in anything else, and right now the fashion is for words that would have turned your great-grandmother's hair white when she was your age. You hear eight-year-old kids on the school grounds using language considered reserved for sailors and mule skinners a few years back.

When the movie *Gone with the Wind* was released, there was a terrible furor over Rhett saying, "Frankly, Scarlett, I don't give a damn." Hard to imagine, isn't it? Back then, "damn" was strong language.

Now we've heard all the four-letter words to the point that they no longer have much meaning. They've lost their force as insults or strong expressions of feeling, and they've gone a step further: They've become a bore. You probably remember some R-rated movies (maybe even X. Shame on you!) in which shock value came from the use of raunchy languge—and also how quickly it got on your nerves. We are thinking of the recent film *48 Hours.* By the time the movie had run ten minutes the use of "that" word had lost any power to shock or startle. It became as irritating as someone whose conversation bristled with "darn."

Instead of ⁹*%–$&–!!* why not try to adopt more individual and expressive ways to state your feelings? People with a flair for words can boil someone in verbal oil or even be as naughty as they like without using a single word you wouldn't say aloud in church. Mae West was a genius at that. She never swore and was never vulgar, but her witty comments (most of which she wrote herself) had audiences gasping even as they broke up laughing and put the censors into a state of cardiac arrest. Nobody is asking you to be such a wizard with words. (*We* should live so long ourselves!) But why not take a crack at it? What have you got to lose except language that is dull? You may gain a reputation as a wit, you will definitely make a better impression on people, and it's fun to play games with language.

Just about the best thing your voice can have going for it, in the long run, is correct use of the English language. We don't mean you need to sound like a BBC announcer; we mean a reasonably knowledgeable use of everyday grammar. "I seen," "he done," "I don't see him no more," "They done went home'' will get you branded with a hick image and not particularly smart at that. Like chewing gum, this one will override everything else.

Learning to speak correctly is not only vital for a good image, but it's also a habit that, once learned, will stay with you for life.

Stacey, describing her first meeting with a group of young people in the town where she was to attend college, said, "This girl was talking with me and she seemed nice and from her clothes I'd have put us in about the same bracket as to background. Then she said, "I seen him coming in. . ." and immediately I was aware of a sharp shift in my feelings. I thought 'She's just a townee, not a college student' and I felt the balance of power shift to me, a superiority on my side. Sounds awful, doesn't it? She was a nice person and all, but before long I was listening with only half an ear to what she was saying and found my attention wandering to other people in the room. She didn't merit my whole focus—I was halfway tuning her out."

Other people have exactly the same reaction, so work on your grammar.

CHAPTER VIII

The Bionic Mouth—and Its Opposite

"It really surprised me when Susan made that comment in class. I was beginning to think the girl couldn't talk; in fact, I don't think I've ever heard her say more than three consecutive words before. Maybe she has a brain after all."

"I'd like to take this to Carrie and get her opinion; after all, she did come up with the idea for the club project. But she'd talk the hind leg off a donkey and I haven't got three hours to waste."

Sound familiar? Everyone has run across people who talk so little that when they do come up with an idea or a worthwhile conversation we are as surprised as if a household pet had decided to hold forth. And certainly we've all met the person who could outtalk a session of Congress with one tonsil tied behind him.

We may not avoid the former, but neither do we give them much credit. When such people do speak up, they often find that their suggestions are ignored, their ideas attract little interest. People have been known to walk several city blocks to keep away from the latter if they don't have several hours to kill. With the bionic mouth, that's everyone else's role—to listen.

Both are people with a handicap. Both often have problems on the job, because (except in relatively rare circumstances) both are vastly underrated. As a general rule both get the scutwork, routine jobs, and are passed over for promotion or not taken seriously when they try to climb the career ladder. Both the nontalker and the bionic mouth find it hard to work in a

51

team effort with other people, and that hurts them in school and on the job.

Both often have problems in their personal relationships, romance now and marriage later. Whether he or she is saying next to nothing, or pouring out enough words to shame a dictionary, the two-way path of real communication is almost completely blocked.

The ugly old stereotype has men and boys as the "strong, silent" species and females as the babblers and yappers, but the fact is that women often have trouble expressing their opinion, speaking up when they want to. And many girls and women become talkative because a male won't: He sits like a lump, and they feel they have to fill the silences.

There are ways to understand why we are like this, and ways to change it.

In many families, there simply isn't a lot of talking. Like the archetypal "New England Yankee," these are people of "few words." They may communicate in words of one syllable, indicate what they want by gestures, and keep their thoughts to themselves. "Babbling" is frowned upon as a sign of weakness and a waste of energy.

Children growing up in such homes tend not to question this; it seems right and normal to them, and they follow and fit into the family pattern. But later they are likely to run into problems. The rest of the world doesn't understand their efforts to communicate with a minimum of verbal expenditure. The rest of the world tends to overlook them, pass them by. Unless they choose someone exactly like themselves (and so pass the pattern along to another generation), they are likely to have problems in serious romance and marriage.

Intelligence isn't necessarily a large factor in how much or how well one talks. Some very bright people aren't verbal or language-oriented. "People who have good verbal ability tend to think that everybody can talk and can express themselves in words if they want to," says C. Eugene Walker, Ph.D., head of a department of psychology at the University of Oklahoma Health Sciences Center. "But this isn't so. I once talked with an engineering student who told me of a required English literature course which involved a lot of poetry. He said he read the poems and could not make any sense of them at all. He concluded that poetry was useless and a fraud. Yet in his own field he was brilliant."

Silent people may also have grown up in homes where there was a great deal of tension and arguing, perhaps even physical fighting. Children not only don't want to draw attention to themselves and so get in the line of fire, they are also painfully aware that they may do or say something to set off the fireworks. So they try to fade into the wallpaper and don't talk.

Bionic mouths, even though they behave exactly the opposite way, often are given the same label as the nontalker: below average in ability, not likely to contribute much to a group or team effort. Such a person often becomes the class or office clown and finds it very difficult to shake the label.

Personal relationships suffer as well. According to Dr. Walker, "The air is full of words, yet they are not communicating anything. Nothing is really being said. A statement to such a person is like opening a floodgate. It sets in motion a barrage of talking, which is actually cutting off communication, not helping it."

Why? Again, the pattern usually starts in childhood.

Children in an "odd man out" spot in the family frequently become bionic mouths. The youngest of several children often has to become a nonstop talker to get and keep attention in the face of the more developed verbal skills of older brothers and sisters. The only girl in a family of boys, or the only boy in a family of girls, sometimes the middle child, sometimes the child who is overshadowed by a better looking or more talented brother or sister may find that constant talking is the only way to be noticed.

Talking may be a nervous reaction or part of a high-strung personality: Like scheherazade, we keep up a steady stream of chatter to keep our heads from being severed, socially. It is also a defense mechanism. "Very insecure people frequently fit into this pattern," Dr. Walker says "Unsure of themselves and very unsure of others, they have found that if they keep talking they are able to control the situation by dominating it and not letting anyone else have a chance to take over. Unfortunately, it also completely eliminates the chance of real communication and usually ends up driving people away."

In your age group and among kids a little younger, being a bionic mouth may be considered an attractive trait—for a while. Most kids are shy when they get to the junior high stage, awkward and unsure of what to do and what to say. When someone else does all the talking, they don't need to. The most popular girls and sometimes the most popular boys at that age are usually the long-distance talkers.

But that changes and you grow up and find you have things to say and know how to say them. By late high school the talkers get on the nerves. Out in the world they may amuse some people, but they rarely do themselves good in college or the business world.

Whether you talk too much, or not enough, you can change. Here are Dr. Walker's recommendations.

Keep in mind that people around you may not be at all helpful to you in your efforts. They are used to you the way you are now, and although your flood of talking may be driving them bonkers, when you try to change you are going to hear, "What's the matter, Caroline, are you sick? You're so *quiet* tonight." If you have been a nontalker, you will find that people are so used to your silence that they interrupt or tune you out, and you may have to stand your ground firmly to make your presence known.

The nontalker should use the technique called "modeling," says Dr. Walker. "Make a detailed analysis of someone you regard as a good conversationalist; not someone whose high voltage personality dominates, but someone who can communicate well with others and in a group of people. Study this person, if possible in a variety of situations. What topics does your 'model' raise? How does he approach them? How does he get other people involved in a conversation? What are some of the phrases he or she uses?"

Construct a similar verbal interchange of your own and try it out on someone. This might be telling a joke well, relating a story, complimenting someone, using a conversation starter that worked for your model. Make a start. Judge the result and make adjustments if necessary. Try again, improving your technique each time. It sounds too simple to work, but we promise you it does. When you are to meet people, plan things to talk about that you feel will interest them. Have a joke or two in mind. Weave what you are saying in with the response of other people. Don't feel that you must barge in with a string of knock-'em-dead one-liners. You are after a good conversation, not a nightclub routine.

Modeling also works with the nonstop talkers. They, too, can gain a great deal not only by the conversational style of someone who is good at the art, but by paying attention to the way such a person relates to those around him or her. "Talkers should learn to relax and make a habit of pausing a few seconds before beginning to speak. Often such people rush into speech before the other person has even finished talking, and the more anxious they become about control of the situation, the more intense their verbalization. If such people can learn to pause and say nothing for a few seconds, relax completely and then begin to talk in a calm and modulated manner, responding directly to what the other person is saying without dragging in a lot of irrelevant side issues, they will soon be using fewer words and communicating much more meaning."

Give yourself a time limit on your speech—say, one minute. At the end of that time you shut up, even if you are in the middle of a word. This technique is often used in therapy; it forces people to weed out needless nattering and get to the point of what they want to say.

You might arrange for a good friend to give you a signal in a social situation, perhaps raising a hand or tugging at an ear, meaning, "You're beginning to sound like an auctioneer; slow down and back off."

Like most attempts to change behavior, this will take time and effort. But stay with it. Every area of your life will benefit.

CHAPTER IX

The Bore War

Most of us would rather be told that our faces would shatter glass and when we enter a room the mice jump up on chairs than to be told we are *boring*.

Unfortunately, bores come in a lot of shapes and sizes. Do you (horrible thought!) fit any of the following categories? Besides the bionic mouth who'd be great on a sailboat if the wind died down, consider the following:

• Sheila, a one-subject bore. Her main interest, almost her *only* interest, is her boyfriend. She can spend three hours on why he decided to change toothpaste brands. Hobbies, your family, a pet hate—anything you go on and on and *ON* about—has the potential to make you a bore.

• Debbie simply isn't "on receive" unless you are talking about something that relates directly to her. She sits with a fixed smile as you talk, and if you suddenly switch the scenario of your great date last night to: "And then we flew to Moscow on a stolen Concorde and bombed the Kremlin, and although we both got shot we thought we were lucky," the glazed look on her face will ease just enough to permit, "Oh, that's great. Sounds like fun."

• Greg has a passion for details so small they cannot be seen with the naked eye. He interrupts conversations—his own and other people's—with: "No, it was Tuesday, not Monday, when it happened. Or was it Friday? It must have been Friday because that's the day that. . ." until everyone else wants to shout "Who *cares?*"

• Charles is outspoken; the Rock of Gibralter is a Jell-O mold compared to the firmness of his opinions. Should you dare to believe differently, Charles is not only determined to change your mind, he'll shout you down trying to do it.

• Elaine sees the world in black and white. She either "just hates" something, or she "just loves" it. "She hacks up a conversation like a meat cleaver," a teacher once said of her. "In fact, she's so cut and dried in her approach to anything that a pleasant conversation with her is almost impossible."

We've all bored someone, on some occasion. No one is fascinating all the time, and you don't need to talk too much to be a bore.

How can you tell if you bore others too often? (Remember, don't place too much reliance on one person's reaction; see if it happens often.) Other people begin to edge away when it appears you're determined to talk, and they avoid eye contact with you. You find that you are talking *at* people, not to them, and comments that should get a response don't. They agree blindly with everything you say: Disagreeing would prolong the conversation, and they don't want that!

Dr. Walker's recommendations for talking too much and too little also work to change the boredom pattern. He suggests that you carefully monitor the other person's reactions. Speak, wait for a response, and in turn respond to that. Don't just keep charging on and on. If the other person sits like a lump and doesn't respond at all, you do the same. Silence won't kill you. Remember that he or she has as much responsibility to keep the conversation going as you have.

Use the modeling techniques, and at first keep your contacts brief. You are less likely to become flustered and blow it, and you can also leave the other person with a more pleasant impression.

Last and perhaps the most important thing of all to change boring behavior: Learn to *listen* to other people. Don't ask questions and then use the replies as a launching pad for your own oratory. If you can really *care* about what they are saying, you are miles ahead of the game.

CHAPTER X

Bigfoot, Abominable Snowmen,
Mermaids, and Lovable Slobs

Somewhere along the pathway of history, perhaps as an offshoot of the beatnik-hippie movement, the notion of the "lovable slob" was born, that neatniks are a pain and sloppy is where it's at.

The perfect example, of course, is *The Odd Couple.* Which one was everyone's favorite and seen in a sympathetic light: fussy, ultra neat Felix or "lovable slob" Oscar?

(Girls and women don't have the same privilege. On us, sloppy is rotten and gains us no points, ever.)

Everyone, unless they have a maid to pick up after them and wash and iron their clothes, has moments of being a slob. If in place of "maid" you put "mother," you ought to be spanked! If you are old enough to read this book and care about your image, you are old enough to clean up after yourself. We believe kids can do a lot to clean up after themselves before they are old enough to read *any* book.

It's easy at your age to look sloppy at times. You have busy lives and a lot to do. More and more mothers work outside the home and tell their kids, "You can operate a washer and dryer and pick up an iron as well as I can; if you want clean clothes, *you* clean 'em!" So nobody can blame you if now and then you look scruffy.

But what is the basic truth about neatniks, slobs, and image?

The truth is simple and plain and it has been proven over and over in tests and studies.

Slobs, the poorly dressed, poorly groomed people, tend to

be discounted, discredited, and overlooked. No one is particularly interested in what they have to say or considers it worth listening to.

There's an interesting example of this in history. When John F. Kennedy and Richard M. Nixon were running for President, they debated each other on television. The contrast in the two men was striking. Kennedy was slim, elegant, in perfectly tailored clothes and groomed to perfection. By contrast Nixon's suit looked ill-fitted and rumpled. His face had a heavy "five o'clock shadow." He didn't look like a man running for the highest office in the land; he looked like someone who had dropped by the studio on his way home from a rotten day at the office. In spite of many things against him, such as being Catholic, as you know Kennedy won, and many people felt that the debates turned the tide.

As mentioned earlier, there are parallels in the animal world. Animals whose coats are shabby and scruffy are marked as easy prey by predators. The animal at the head of the pecking order is always the best groomed of the herd or flock. A circling coyote won't come near the "boss" horse or cow of a herd. He chooses victims that look as if they can't fight back.

So it is with humans.

Sloppiness says, "I'm not even able to take care of myself, so don't expect me to be able to do much else."

What marks you as a slob, the kind whom others overlook and tune out?

- Zits and a generally poor complexion.
- Dirty, unkempt hair. If your hair doesn't look too good even right after washing, consider changing shampoos; you may see a big difference right away.
- Four or five layers of makeup. We don't mean too much makeup, but rather what is obviously one layer from yesterday and one from last night, iced over with a fresh batch from this

morning. The face can look as many-layered as an onion, and that defeats the whole purpose of makeup. One looks worse, not better.

• Wrinkled, scruffy looking clothes. One cliché of our youth is still true: "You don't have to be rich to look neat and clean. Anyone can afford soap and water and the electricity to run an iron." We think a lot of the "last week's wash" look is the result of everything's being labeled "permanent press." Whatever the label says, the garment that can come out of the dryer and go right on your back, looking great, is rare. Almost everything needs a touch of the iron, to smooth down the cuffs, make the collar stop looking like roofing material, polish the button placket in front. Okay, if you think it's too much trouble and not that important, it's your choice. But you are going to be outdistanced by the people who do think it's that important and are willing to expend a little energy in their own behalf.

• Ragged, dirty fingernails that look as if you've just clawed your way up the side of a six-story building. Your hands are in view much more than you realize. Boys as well as girls need to stay manicured.

• Boys who don't have a clean shave. This looks worse on boys than on older men because at your age the hair is more patchy; you look as if you've got dirt on your face.

• Dingy, yellow-gray teeth. Bad breath. No deodorant. Nauseaville.

• The coming-apart-at-the-seams look: Button off the shirt. Button off the waistband of the pants or skirt and a safety pin in its place. Hem on skirt or pants coming down. Seam of a sleeve beginning to unravel. Slip or bra strap held by a safety pin. People like this leave other people with the uneasy feeling that a gust of wind would leave them totally nude.

• Sloppy and inappropriate clothing worn "because I hate dressing up; I don't want to bother." This include such things as jeans and a T-shirt worn to a funeral, or sweats at a party because "they're comfortable and no trouble," or tennis shoes and an OP at a family wedding because "I don't really know them that well and didn't want to go to all the trouble."

People who dress like that are making a very strong statement: They are saying loud and clear, "I don't care what is appropriate or looks right or will make people glad they invited me; the only thing that matters to me is what *I* want, and I want to be comfortable and not go to any trouble because to me you aren't worth it." Nice, eh?

If you insist on clothing that conveys that image, be prepared for the results. Your image is as offensive as if you had it printed on a sign around your neck.

• Skid Row special shoes: no polish for the last year and a half, split seams, and run-over heels. If you can't bring yourself to take care of your shoes, wear plastic ones. But again, unless plastic shoes are designed to shout "Genuine Plastique!" they not only look plastic, they look cheap. They can also slaughter your feet.

• Inappropriate clothing on heavy people. The girl in a tube top with a spare tire bulging out above and below it. The guy with the big stomach and the T-shirt that doesn't quite come down to his jeans, so bystanders are treated to the sight of his rolling belly with the navel occasionally heaving into view. It's sort of like being stared at by a cyclops.

• The guy, or girl, in a Magnum-type Hawaiian shirt and plaid pants. As proved by some clothes currently for sale, at prices designed to harden the arteries, even the big-name designers can't get away with a combination like that. Done by a haute couture French designer or assembled by someone color blind in a closet where the light had burned out, mixed patterns are almost always ghastly.

• The thin girl in clothes miles too big for her. She's wearing a sun dress that she could turn around in. She gives you the awful feeling that with one wrong move the dress will fall right off. This baggy, unkempt look says, "Poor, pathetic, inadequate me!"

• The girl in the T-shirt pulled over the waistband of a corduroy skirt, which is too long and worn with tennis shoes. She looks as if someone had thrown her clothes on her with a pitchfork. The effect: Tobacco Road and terrible.

Unfortunately, if you want some wonderful examples of terrible clothes, you can find them in shops where a slip can cost $150.

Recently one of the authors was accompanied to a high-fashion show by a slightly apprehensive but curious male friend. The designer featured was Japanese, and the clothes had been hailed by the fashion press as "the most innovative new ideas in years."

They might have been that; they were also hideous. The colors seemed to have been inspired by mud and made even the prettiest models' complexions look bad, and the shoulder pads made the models look almost deformed. Among the outfits were little numbers like plaid highwater pants over pantyhose printed with the enormous cabbage roses you find in Victorian wallpaper and some that might have been hacked out of lengths of cloth with a broken beer bottle and hung on the models with tape. As we left, this was the conversation:

"Well, what did you think of it?"

"Can you wait a minute for my answer? I'm still in a state of shock."

"Would you pay $1,200 for one of those numbers?"

"Pay $1,200 for it! I wouldn't have the nerve to be alone in the same room with it!"

"I can see why jeans stay so popular."

"The Japanese are still mad at us over World War II, huh?"

You can be a slob on any price tag.

CHAPTER XI

Families and Images

Earlier we said that it might be less than a good idea to tell family members that you are making an effort to change your image. The plain truth is that, where your own individual image is concerned, your family can be a big problem.

They rarely mean to be. Almost never is it intentional. But it is very common, very real, and often very hard to handle, on your part and on theirs, if you are trying to break away from an image that hurts.

At this point your image is probably pretty much the same as your family's. If you try to change, there's an excellent chance they will see it as a rejection of themselves and their values.

Let's take an example. You're a young man and you've decided you want to become a banker or a stockbroker and that you have brains and ability in that field. Your father is a blue-collar worker whose life has always been pretty much a money struggle. Certainly he'd like you to do well in life and not have the problems he has had.

And yet, deep inside, he may also resent your choice of a career field.

How often have your heard a man say, "Well, I'm raising my boy to follow in my footsteps." If you have ever thought of being the father of a boy, haven't you also thought, "I'd want to raise him to be like me?" Even when men and boys don't say that, almost all of them think it. And since nearly every man has something of those feelings, to find that his son wants to head off in an entirely new direction can be a jolt. Many men—many parents—see it not only as a rejection but as unspoken criticism: "What's the matter, is what I am not good enough for you? Is there some other man you'd rather be like? Is that it?"

Remember the scene from *Huckleberry Finn* when Huck's drunken Pap goes after Huck for learning to read and curses people for "raising up a boy to be better then his father"? Men who are nothing at all like "Pap" can still, deep down, have something of the same feelings.

Such feelings rarely come out into the open. Most of the time parents aren't even aware that they exist; they only know that your efforts to change your image "get on their nerves" or seem wasted and silly. If you know that dressing like a preppy in the affluent look is going to help you get a job or do better in school, you are still likely to hear, "Well, look at Uncle So-and-So; and look how well he's done and how much money he's made!" There is an Uncle So-and-So in every family. Bully for them! But they are exceptions, not examples to follow, in most cases. To repeat ourselves, you are facing a rougher world, so stack the deck in your favor. Give yourself every advantage.

Your family may resist your efforts to improve your image with "teasing." "Well, here comes Little Lord Fauntleroy!" or "Oh, like your new shirt! Wall Street will probably offer you a million a year to work there now."

Such "teasing" is the verbal equivalent of dirty alley fighting. It's one of the nastier things people do to each other without drawing blood. Someone can say the meanest, most cutting and hurtful things, and if you respond by being angry and hurt, they come back with "Hey, I was just teasing. Can't you take a joke? Don't be so blasted touchy!" That is the perfect double put-down. They have got in the deep cut *and* made you seem petty and in the wrong because you didn't like it. We go into this in detail for a reason: "Teasing" is a favorite family weapon against something they can't oppose openly without looking petty and in the wrong themselves, so be on the watch for it.

Families aren't the only ones. "Friends," especially if you seem to be going in different directions from them, are good at it as well.

How do you handle it?

The best general way is to ignore it as much as possible. If you blow up, get angry or defensive, respond in any definite way—especially if it makes you look bad—you will come off looking and feeling worse than whoever is giving you a hard time.

So the best response is no response at all. Like a joke that falls flat, "teasing" makes the teaser look silly if all it gets is the halibut eye from you. Let silence stretch out to the point where it becomes uncomfortable, then flatly change the subject and keep it changed. It will probably take several times to make a difference, but it is the best way to handle such a situation.

Your parents belong to a somewhat more enlightened generation than those before it, so you aren't quite so likely to face such a problem. But you might, and it's something to be alert for and ready to cope with should it arise.

We have written this chapter mainly for boys, since this kind of possessiveness is rarer with girls. On the contrary, many families *want* their daughters to improve their image because it is seen as helping them to marry up the social and economic ladder. If a daughter wants to break away and go into an entirely different field from the traditional—become an astronaut, a jockey, a politician, or whatever other than the stereotypic nurse or teacher—she may face an equally hairy set of problems, but they don't especially have to do with image.

She (and he) should be aware, however, that entering an entirely different field is likely to be something the right image can help.

CHAPTER XII

Coloring Your Image

As most girls reading this probably know, the big thing right now is "having your colors done," having a consultant tell you what colors look well on you and what don't. Is it worth it, paying money to have this done?

Maybe. Like so many things that suddenly are a big business—especially in the fashion industry—some companies are excellent at this and other companies, or individuals, don't know the first thing about what they are doing.

Some of you, probably the boys in particular, may say that color analysis is nonsense. You aren't alone. In Helen Gurley Brown's book *Having It All,* she says: "We [*Cosmopolitan* magazine] ran an article on what colors to wear. . .we should have been arrested! The best expert on what colors are best for you is you!" Well, Mrs. Brown is a smart woman and right on a lot of things, but on that particular issue she's so far off base that she isn't even in the ballpark.

"You" aren't the best expert on yourself in more than one out of two thousand cases. If ever there was an example of not being able to see ourselves as others see us, it's in choosing colors that are best for us. And yet the right colors can make a 300 percent difference in how well you look!

So we think it is well worth the money to have your colors done—for boys and men as well as us ladies—*but* it should be done by someone who has had the right training and who has the "artist's eye" for it. One consultant we know told four women—a blonde with sallow skin, a woman whose parents had come from southern Italy and who was very dark, a woman with light brown hair and pale skin, and a woman with dark brown hair and a medium-dark tan—that they were all "summers" and should wear about the same colors. That is not only silly, but a waste of money.

Unless you have money to waste (and who does these days?), find a consultant who represents a company that gives its people extensive training, who uses many colors (several hundred, we recommend) to compare, and who is recommended by someone whose judgment you trust or on whom you can see fantastic results.

One of the authors found such a company (it was on the expensive side), which analyzed not only color but fashion type. When I had got all the mistakes out of my closet, it might have belonged to Lady Godiva. You could yell in there and get an echo! But the results were wonderful: It's the smartest money I ever spent on myself!

You probably know two or three colors that generally look well on you. But until you can have your colors analyzed, here's a basic guide for you.

Human skin, except for the very darkest, is of two base tones—pink and yellow—and you may be totally wrong in trying to judge which is yours. To tell, look at the palm of your hand. On most of us it's a pink-red. Now, with your thumb, press the center of your palm. When you take your thumb away, what is the base color of the light spot? If you aren't sure, try doing it with your hand against a yellow background, and then a pink background. Which seems most like the color of your skin before it returns to its normal, usually rather mottled, reddish-pink color?

Whatever is your base color, you will almost certainly look best in colors that harmonize with it. If your skin is yellow-based, then reds and pinks are almost certain to look ghastly on you. If it is pink-toned, you are likely to look awful in shades of yellow and orange.

What does your best color have to do with your image? A lot. Remember, the better you look, the better the overall image you project. A thunderingly wrong color may leave people with a negative, unpleasant reaction to you, even though they may have no idea why they feel that way.

Color has other image aspects as well.

Black is not the best color on many people. (Oddly enough, both authors, who are totally different in coloring and type, have black as a "best color." The author who is a model, walking through a store or shop in black velvet, is like a comet with a tail of customers wanting to know how much and in what department the garment is sold.) Black also leaves a negative image if it is worn very frequently. A person who dresses in black constantly is seen as being neurotic and morbid, or affected and phony, or trying to convey an impression of menace and threat. He or she may achieve a temporary "macho" or "seductress" image, but in the long run it won't get you very far in life. So use all-black carefully, for when you really want it to count, not all the time.

White is supposed to be an easy color to wear, but actually it is not. Pure white doesn't look well on many people, and it can make you look tired and drawn even when you aren't. Did you ever notice how tired doctors and nurses often look. It doesn't come with the job; it's the white uniforms most of the time.

Girls have probably heard it said that everyone can wear pastels. It's a favorite ploy of sales people when pastels are "the" colors for a season. Well, don't be fooled: Pastels are very hard to wear. They tend to be particularly disastrous on someone whose complexion isn't the greatest, accenting muddiness, blotchiness, or the mottled look that acne can leave. And they are, almost without exception, second rate in image.

Go through stores in the richer and the poorer parts of town and ntoice the colors they stock. Chances are you will be surprised.

In the expensive stores colors tend to be sharp and clear, and sometimes strong. In the bargain stores colors are often a blend: yellow-green, red-orange, the blue-green known as aqua. Check around; you'll see what we mean.

Prints, again, are tricky and are likely to impart a second-rate image. Princess Diana wears a lot of prints and can get away with them, but she's a rarity. The same dress on her much less attractive mother-in-law or her sister-in-law Princess Anne? Frump city. Again, you can see what we mean in stores at opposite ends of the scale. Prints in the rich part of town are rare and tend to be dark-colored and muted in tone. Prints in the "nothing over $5" stores may make you feel you could get a suntan from them, they are so bright.

Most of the time we harmonize with ourselves in coloring; hair, eyes, and skin are shades that blend. But not always. We've all seen people whose coloring looked as if Mother Nature had had an attack of color blindness. Redheads, alas, are most often the victims, with orangy-red hair and pinky-red skin that totally clash. A friend, stuck with such a combination, says it usually goes with "nothing-colored eyes and albino lashes and eyebrows." True—unfortunately. There is also the washed-out blonde with pinky skin. As we have said before, these things have nothing to do with your real brains and ability. But they don't give others the impression that you have brains or ability, and so you may never get a chance to show them.

What if you are stuck with coloring that doesn't work?

You don't have to take it, even from Mother Nature.

So—cheat.

Hair coloring is cheap and—contrary to what your grandmother has probably said—won't "ruin" your hair if you select the right kind and use it properly.

In possible, have your hair colored first by a professional, because it's easy to make a mistake yourself. For example, browns can shade toward yellow, red, or gray, and the wrong tone can be almost as big a disaster as a wrong color you are stuck with. So let a professional start you off. Don't, however, let yourself be conned into believing that only a pro can color your hair, as some hairdressers will try to do. (Unless you have big bucks: This is an *expensive* process.) Choose a color you can reproduce with something from the drugstore or supermarket.

Is your reaction, "Oh, I wouldn't have the nerve to do that—if I went to school with my hair dyed they'd laugh me out?"

Certainly there is likely to be some initial teasing and people giving you a hard time. But which is worse: one hassle that will soon end, or a continued poor image caused by coloring problems? You might change your hair over the summer, or do it very gradually. Either way is likely to let you ease into a new role with less trauma than if you did a sudden about-face during a school year.

"Albino eyelashes" and brows, such as our friend described, are also a handicap, in that they make eyes seem to disappear. Girls know what to do about it. Boys should be aware that eyelashes and eyebrows can be dyed to make them darker and that look is almost sure to be an improvement for you.

A word—or several words—of caution here.

DON'T TRY TO DO THIS YOURSELF!

It's a job for a professional. You could go blind trying it yourself. People have. So don't even think of such a thing. Go to a professional salon and have it done with ingredients that have been tested and proved safe.

Eyes are almost always the right color for you—with one exception. Very light-colored eyes, especially if the rest of your coloring is on the cool side, sometimes look cold and flinty. You can probably think of people who fit this category. It's unfortunate, because people may react to you, and expect you to be, very different from what you really are.

As you probably know, colored contact lenses are available now, and, while not cheap, they are not totally out of reach.

Should you get lenses only to change the color of your eyes?

We asked several optometrists and received varying answers—"Certainly" to "No." According to Lois Kenner, assistant to Oklahoma City optometrist Curtis Roberson, "That's not surprising, there are still a few optometrists who barely believe in contact lenses! But we have fitted patients with lenses just for the color, and usually they look better and feel better about themselves."

The negative image of "cold" eyes has made an impression on at least one company. Dr. Roberson and Ms. Kenner are taking part in a study testing lavender and orange lenses on patients. "No, you don't look as if you are practicing for Halloween," she said. "Those are basically warm colors; rather than changing the color of your eyes, they 'warm' the color you have and give you a look to which people respond more positively. The lenses are still in the test stage and haven't been released by the FDA yet, but I feel they probably will be before long."

Orange lenses may actually seem tame. "One company came out with some that were star-shaped!" Ms. Kenner said. "Talk about bizarre-looking!"

CHAPTER XIII

Diet Is A Four-Letter Word

If you are a teen with a weight problem—if you are *anyone* with a weight problem—you have probably been preached at and nagged on the subject of losing weight. As anyone knows who has faced such a problem, it isn't easy to overcome.

Yet we keep trying, sometimes in the most ridiculous ways.

Someone once said, "If you want to have a guaranteed best seller, write a book promising that the reader can eat like a pig and still lose ten pounds a day. If doesn't matter how ridiculous your diet is, the book will sell!" True. Just look at the tabloids on the newspaper racks. They make a good part of their income on diets.

And the latest diet pills! A while back the big thing was "starch blockers" that supposedly let you eat ten pounds of potatoes and not feel a calorie. Right now it's grapefruit pills and a magical substance that "burns fat off while you sleep."

Well, the unfortunate truth is that there is no miracle that will peel the weight off while your back is turned. *You* have to do it, and it takes effort.

Also unfortunately, people your age are the world's dumbest about nutrition and the biggest suckers (sorry, it's the only term that fits) for fad diets and "miracle" cures for weight problems. Most of them don't work, and some are outright dangerous. A few of them are killers.

One of the authors collaborated on *Coping with Medical Emergencies* and has seen more than one teenager come into an emergency room in serious condition from a fad diet or a too-extreme crash diet. An acquaintance of hers went on a crash diet that she made up herself. Within a few days the woman began behaving strangely. She was agitated, suspicious, paranoid, and hyperactive. Then she began hallucinating and wound up in a psychiatric ward.

She was released within a week. The doctors concluded that she had not had a genuine psychotic episode, but that her diet was the cause of her going off the rails. As one physician put it, "She had her electrolytes, her basic body chemistry, so screwed up it's a wonder she was thinking as straight as she was. Junking up your body and brain like that and expecting them to work right is like expecting a car to run on peanut butter!"

The woman recovered with no aftereffects, but she was lucky. People—most of them young people—have died as the result of idiot diets.

So go at losing the right way and the smart way. That's the way to make the pounds get off and stay off.

To make a diet work you need the right attitude, the right "mind-set." If we knew a formula that would work for everyone, we'd be so rich we wouldn't talk to Gloria Vanderbilt. We can only tell you what seems to work best for the most people.

To begin with, *don't* try to lose weight for a special occasion, such as an upcoming party, or for a special person—"If I lose ten pounds I just know that hunk in the next seat in English will ask me out," or "If I lose thirty pounds I'll bet that cute girl whose locker is next to mine will notice me." Keep such things in mind as possibilities when you lose, but don't make them the main goal.

There are two reasons for this. First, you need to lose weight for *yourself*. As the commercial says, "You're worth it." You deserve it, you are entitled to a slender body and all that goes with that great look and feeling.

Second, if things don't work out as you planned—the hunk doesn't notice, the cute girl looks right through you—you feel a failure. You feel that you gave up all those lovely calories for nothing. That reinforces the negative feelings that people with a weight problem have about themselves. So don't fall into the trap.

The mind-set for beginning a diet is when you are feeling good about something. Get happy—*then* start cutting down on what you eat. Get wrapped up in a project, join a club, start a new hobby. You'll not only feel good, you'll have something to occupy your mind and your time when you start to think of food.

The reverse—beginning a diet when you are on a downer, like right after a breakup—is just awful! Most of us eat more when we are miserable, so you are making something that is hard anyway twice as difficult. Don't do it. Get over the worst of your blues, then begin to cut calories when you are excited about something else. It works a lot better that way.

We don't have any specific diet in mind. We do recommend, if you need to lose over fifteen pounds, that you see your doctor before you begin. He or she might have some helpful advice for you.

Other than that, you don't need a special "diet." You know pretty well what is fattening and what isn't; it doesn't take a genius to see that. Following are some ideas to help you avoid what is:

• Be honest about your reactions to food. Don't say to yourself, "I'll go with the gang for pizza but I'll stick to the salad bar," if you know darn well that you won't, that the delicious smells and the sight of everyone else digging into pizza will be too much. Just avoid it altogether. Sure, you may miss some good times with friends while you are dodging calories; just tell yourself you'll make it up later.

• When the school lunch is a high-calorie favorite, brown-bag it for the day and eat outside. Don't expose yourself to temptation until you build the will to resist it.

• Don't set your sights too high. If you are a dress size 18, don't set your only goal as a size 6, or if you wear size 46 pants, don't say you are going to a 28-inch waist. As we said, too-high goals not only are almost sure to fail, but give you a built-in excuse for not reaching them.

• Set intermediate goals, a size 16 dress or a 42-inch waist. When you get there, give yourself a reward (and we don't mean food). Get something new and great to wear, perhaps, or do something you have really wanted to. Take an introductory flying lesson. Rent a horse from a stable and go for a ride.

You might even keep a notebook record of your progress. Enter your present weight and below it increments of five or ten pounds, depending on what you want to lose. Beside each write the date of reaching that goal. When you start the book, scatter through it points of reward; for example, when you reach 140 pounds you will buy yourself something at such and such a store.

Do keep rewards—nonfood rewards—in mind. It doesn't work to give up, give up, give up and never get anything in return. At first even a gradually slimming body may not seem enough for the sacrifices you have made. So give yourself other, tangible rewards; they will help to make it seem worthwhile.

• Drink plenty of water. Eight glasses a day will not only be good for you, but they help to fill the empty stomach. *And* you will probably find that you feel better, your skin looks better, your eyes and hair are shinier, as you go. Cutting out food that is bad for you has a lot more benefits than just dropping pounds.

• If you know your willpower is shaky, put off eating. There is a lot to be said for procrastination at certain times. You'll have the hamburger—but not right now. You'll have it for dinner instead of lunch. Or you'll have it tomorrow. Or you'll wait until the weekend when you can really relax and enjoy it. Eventually you'll eat it, but you'll have bypassed a lot of calories in the meantime.

• Learn to love salad bars. It takes *seventeen* salads to do as much damage as *one* thick slice of cake with heavy icing or cream filling. And too-rich foods can make you feel logy and bloated; salads never do. A lot of kids don't like salads. They say, "I'm a meat and potatoes person." Salads can be an acquired taste, so put a little effort into acquiring it; we promise it will be well worth it. Since some of the fast-food chains have the best salad bars in town, you can get a terrific meal for not much money and very few calories. Try putting on your favorite things plus a few things you either don't like or have never tried (mushrooms, maybe) and a favorite low-calorie dressing. We'd bet the ranch before long you will be hooked, too.

Last, when you are seriously tempted, try aversion therapy. Tell yourself that you are going to give in and eat whatever is driving you bonkers, but first spend five minutes—five *full* minutes—thinking of that thing, picturing it, in revolting circumstances. Covered with grubby gray-green mold. (Ugh!) Wet and collapsing and soggy. Covered with sand or kitty litter. With spiders crawling all over it. Having just been fished out of a cage full of pythons. Whatever makes your skin crawl, use that. Before long you will probably find that the mere idea of eating the thing makes you feel queasy.

The "miracle" of miracle diets is generally how fast they make the inventors rich. So don't fall for them. Losing weight, particularly a lot of weight, is hard work and takes effort. But hang in there. Give it your best shot.

You are worth it.

CHAPTER XIV

Slice, Cut, Stitch

There is probably no one who hasn't stared into the mirror at an unfavorite feature and thought, "Oh, if only I could have a plastic surgeon fix that, life would be great!" But not many of us actually go so far as to consult a plastic surgeon about our problem.

Should you? Let's consider the possibilities.

At one time, plastic surgery for young people was considered a ridiculous idea. If you had a real problem feature, you were told to wait until you were older to have it fixed, "when it's more important to you." But, as we have pointed out all along, much of your personality and the pattern of your future are being set now, and we believe that if it's important enough to fix, it's important enough to fix *now*. According to P. S. Bajaj, M.D., a reconstructive and cosmetic surgeon at Oklahoma City's St. Anthony Hospital, "If a youngster has a problem, it is far better to repair it before other children begin to tease him and give him a bad time, and make him—or her—shy and unsure. I do many procedures on children before they start to school. While there are some things, such as rhinoplasty [a nose job] that can't be done before the middle to late teens, I think the sooner a problem is corrected, the better."

Parents don't always agree.

One big reason is costs. Cosmetic surgery may be covered by insurance, depending on the nature of the problem and how the claim is filled out; some wording will get you by, other ways of stating the problem won't. But if you are thinking of cosmetic surgery, it's better to face the fact that you might have to pay for the whole thing and "up front," before you are even admitted to the hospital.

There are many procedures, however, that are done on an "outpatient" basis. - You check into the hospital, have the procedure done, and go home the same day. That is a tremendous cost saver.

How important will such a surgical procedure be to you? Teens who really could benefit from it rarely choose to have an operation just to make them "better-looking." Let's consider four teen-agers whose problems did warrant cosmetic surgery and see what happened to them.

Steve was thirteen, bright, had an easy going personality, and was the son of a wealthy oilman. Although he was generally easy to get along with, all through school his teachers had had degrees of negative reaction to him. Other people he met reacted the same way. They seemed on the defensive, ready to get angry, unwilling to answer questions at length. Steve had never given any thought to why; he just accepted it as being "the way things are."

Then a friend of his mother, who had never met him, saw his school picture and asked, "What's he mad about?"

The mother was surprised. "He's not mad about anything. Why?"

"Well, when my son has his lip pushed out like that he's furious and pouting about something."

Steve's mother looked again at the picture and realized something: Steve's upper lip was average in size, but his lower lip was extremely wide and rather thick. It was an inherited trait, exactly like his father's and younger brothers', so no one in the family had considered it unusual. But now his mother showed the photo to a few more people who didn't know Steve and got the same reaction: He looks mad; he looks as if he's sulking about something. She decided this might be causing Steve more problems than anyone realized.

Steve admitted that he was sometimes teased about his lip, but he had the kind of personality that just let it roll off; he truly wasn't bothered by the kidding of people his own age. But the thought of getting along better with teachers sounded good to him. So he and his parents consulted a cosmetic surgeon.

The doctor agreed that Steve's pouty lip probably wasn't helping him get along in the world, and he explained the operation that would reduce it to match its partner.

Tracy, at sixteen, had a generally poor school record, few friends, and a list of problems that included vague illnesses, outbursts of crying and depression over practically nothing, and increasing withdrawal from other people. Tracy hated her looks, without saying exactly why, so much that she didn't even wear makeup, saying, "What's the use? I'd still be ugly."

One evening as the family was watching television, a report was given on children with Down's syndrome (mongolism). "That looks just like Tracy," her younger, bratty, and very pretty sister giggled. Tracy was horrified and very upset, but alone in her room she realized that her sister was right. Tracy had inherited from her mother's side of the family a thick pad of fat under each eye that gave her a sleepy, "dim-witted" look. As a child she had been called "Retardo" by some of her classmates. People shied away from her as many of us do from people with a handicap—but in this case a handicap that didn't exist.

Tracy went on her own to see a reconstructive and cosmetic surgeon and was told that the problem could be corrected, but her parents went up in smoke at the idea and at the cost. Tracy had suffered a great deal because of this one feature, however, and she was determined to have it changed. She went to work at any kind of job she could get, from baby-sitting to heavy housecleaning, banking every cent possible. When her parents realized that she was serious and also understood better the emotional cost of Tracy's "half-wit eyes," as she called them, they told her that if she could raise half the amount needed, they would come up with the other half.

Tracy talked to the doctor, who suggested several ways they might lower the costs. She also reduced her own fee a bit. A month before school started in the fall, Tracy had her operation.

Rick had gone through all fifteen years of life being called "Dumbo," "Jughead," or "Alfred E. Neumann." His ears weren't especially large, but they stuck out like two wide-open doors on a car. Since such ears are traditionally part of the caricature of someone really dense, Rick found he was often considered not very bright.

(There may be even a royal illustration of this particular image bugaboo. Many people have said of Prince Charles that he is "no mental giant," "not especially intelligent." The Prince also has ears that stick out. He may not care to sit and discuss Shakespeare or the modern-day application of Greek drama, but anyone who can fly a helicopter, as the future king does, is definitely smarter than the average bear.)

Rick was another teen who didn't have the support of his parents on the idea of "pin his ears back" surgery, but he also worked and made the money on his own.

Michelle at sixteen was a slender blonde who would have been extremely pretty if, as she put it, "I'd got only *my* nose instead of three other people's as well." Her nose was long and had a bulbous knob on the end of it. She was so self-conscious about her looks, so unsure of herself, and so wounded by the teasing of schoolmates that she had seriously considered becoming a nun, "not because I believe that way, just to get away from people."

Michelle's family couldn't afford the relatively expensive

rhinoplasty, but when Michelle received a small inheritance from her grandmother she made an appointment with a cosmetic surgeon and discovered that her legacy would just cover the cost of the operation.

Her parents objected. They wanted her to save the money for college, and at first they refused to give permission for the operation. Both the doctor and a counselor at Michelle's school talked with them, however, and in the end they agreed.

In Michelle's emotional state, college loomed not as a goal, but as a nightmare. The counselor pointed out one other aspect of her physical problem that would never have occurred to her parents. She said that among girls who were promiscuous and became unwed mothers, a high percentage considered themselves ugly and had a poor self-image. "They are so withdrawn they'll respond to almost any boy who shows an interest. They give themselves because they think they can't hold a boyfriend any other way and don't have anything else to offer. They keep their baby often, because 'At least it will love me, even if no one else does.'"

What happened to these four? The change in their lives was definite and very much for the better. Steve was perhaps the least affected; his problem had not been very severe, and he had a personality that could generally handle it. The change in Michelle was the most marked. "She has become a totally different girl," her mother said. "Her grades have gone up, she's in a good mood most of the time, happy, singing around the house, interested in all kinds of new things. She has a very nice boyfriend and is joining a lot of things at school. It wasn't like a nose job she had, it was like a personality transplant."

Cosmetic, reconstructive, or plastic surgery (more and more such surgeons are rejecting the term "plastic") was once viewed only as "vanity" surgery, performed to augment the bustlines or lift the faces of the rich and conceited. Many people still see it in that light. But for these four teens and many other people like them, it is more than an operation on the body: it is surgery that changes their soul.

Of course, not all cosmetic surgery makes such a great difference. Sometimes it truly isn't needed; a physical feature is blamed for troubles that have their roots elsewhere. Reputable doctors talk to such patients about why a procedure is wanted and try to find out if that is really the source of difficulty or if something else is at the root of the trouble.

Another, less extensive and expensive, type of surgery that is done in the doctor's office and can make a world of difference in one's looks and image is the removal of warts and moles.

One of the authors has a young friend who is very striking looking in an unusual way. She has terrific taste in clothes and has been a runway model, but up close she puts people off. On her chin and on the side of her jaw are two enormous red moles. As one young man put it, "When I talk to her I find myself staring at that mole on her chin and watching it wag up and down. It's terrible!"

Why won't she have them removed? "I'm not about to let anyone go sticking needles in my face!"

Moles are ugly. Moles say second rate. Can you imagine the chairman of the board of a big corporation with an enormous mole on his nose? A successful woman doctor with a "wicked witch of the west" mole on her chin? Probably not. We certainly can't.

Moles are also extremely aging, a fact to keep in mind for later on in your life.

What is involved in the removal of a mole? The area is prepped (scrubbed with antiseptic) and then a local anesthetic is given. Yes, that is the needle in your face. It stings, sometimes very sharply, for three to five seconds. Count to five. Surely you aren't such a baby you can't stand something stinging that long! Then there is no feeling at all. The mole is removed by cautery (burning, which sounds far worse than it is) or by an incision, in which case there will probably be a stitch or two. Stitches itch for a day or two, but that's all there is to it. If you can't stand to see the needle moving in your direction, shut your eyes and don't look. If you are really in a panic at the thought, ask for a tranquilizer.

Be prepared for questions about the bandage on your face. One of the authors once had a small black mole on the tip of her nose removed. It required a stitch and the bandage kept falling off, and for three or four days people kept saying, "Hey, there's a bug on your nose!" But it was better than having a mole there.

If you have moles, have them taken off. You'll feel and look better.

What if your parents are totally opposed to the idea of cosmetic surgery? Or you, or they, can't afford it?

The day will come when you will be on your own and not need parental permission. You might start a savings account now for that future time.

As one girl said, "My parents have a fit when I say I want my nose fixed. From the side it isn't all that bad, but from the front it looks as if someone hit me with a brick. It's wide and thick and sort of spreads over my face. When I am old enough I am going to have it changed, and I've started saving for that, even though my parents tell me I'm too self-conscious about it. They don't feel the things I feel because of it! But until I can have something done, just knowing that it's going to happen sometime has made a lot of difference to me. I'm more outgoing now, more optimistic and hopeful. I see things from a happier point of view, and that alone has made a lot of difference to me."

A final comment regarding image and its effect. Get an old album cover and look at the pictures of "the Jackson 5" and especially of the youngest brother as a boy of eight or nine. Do you think Michael Jackson would have the success, the image and the following he does now, if he still had the nose he had back then?

CHAPTER XV

Overcoming a Bad First Impression

We've always heard how important it is to make a good first impression, and nobody really doubted it. But recent psychological studies have discovered that it can be even more important than we used to think. In today's busy, hectic world, the person who makes a poor first impression may find that he or she is always thereafter considered in that light. He stumbled over his own feet the first time he met you: He is therefore a klutz. She gave a somewhat ridiculous answer the first day in class, and to the busy, harried teacher she is never seen as capable of much else. The first time you met in a social situation he sat there like a bump on a log and didn't say a word: He is boring and wouldn't be interesting to know. It's very unfair that this happens, but it certainly does happen.

How do you overcome a bad first impression? According to family therapist Bob Gardenhire, there are two main lines to take, internal and external.

"First, spend some time trying to figure out why you did that," Gardenhire recommends. "Were you having a bad day? Were you angry at yourself or someone else? Just not with it? Really worried about something?

"Or is it possible that your expectations were too high? Often it becomes too important that we make a good impression, or we are intimidated by a teacher, an employer, someone of the opposite sex whom we want to impress. So we get tense, uptight, and can't get out an intelligent sentence or stand on our own feet. Consider those possibilities; they will help you get the whole episode in better perspective."

Sometimes, because of these too-high expectations, our first impression wasn't as bad as we thought. Time will take its course and smooth out the worst social bombs.

"You might get a better view of the situation by calling a friend and talking it over, asking 'Did I come off as bad as it seemed to me?' or if it's fitting for the situation, 'Do you think I still have a chance after that?'" Gardenhire recommends.

If you really came off bad and there's no doubt about it, he suggests you meet the barrier head-on (and that can be difficult to do.) Say, "I was a complete turkey—klutz—space cadet—dimwit—or whatever, and I'm really not like that. Let's pretend it never happened and go back to square one, okay?"

He also suggests that you consider making a peace offering of some sort, a gesture small and not overdone, saying, "Your friendship or your good opinion is important to me, and I do want you to think well of me."

"Be able to laugh at yourself if you did something outrageous, but—as with the peace offering—don't overdo it. Protesting too much just reinforces the other person's impression that that is after all the real you."

Don't be afraid to point up a good, positive thing you have done that overcomes the bad thing—a particularly good piece of work in class, for instance. Again, use the light touch, don't run it into the ground; just point up to the other person that it wasn't the real you who messed things up that once.

"Resolve to be different," Gardenhire recommends. "Sometimes bad first impressions are the result of simple carelessness, or of negative feelings about yourself. Work on building a good inner image of yourself. This does show on the outside. [What we've been saying all along.]

"Above all, don't be hard on yourself for making a mistake. *Everyone* blows it once in a while."

CHAPTER XVI

When a Poor Self-Image Is Caused by Someone Else

So far we have talked mostly about image problems and uncertainties that are just a part of growing up and finding out who you are. Now we are going to tackle something much more unpleasant, but also something that many teens are stuck with: when something someone else is doing is feeding a poor self-image.

Most of us, at the early junior high stage, were dissatisfied with our looks and certain we were doomed to a hermitic existence and failure in life because we didn't look like teen versions of Tom Selleck or Christie Brinkley. We grow out of that as we get our feet on the ground as people and gain some confidence in ourselves as we are.

A bad head trip from someone else we tend not to grow out of. Many people carry those emotional scars to the grave.

Karen's younger brother had picked on her since both were tiny. He called Karen a "big pig" because she had a slight weight problem, laughed and jeered at her when she tried to do something and failed, felt free to go to her room and take things without asking, and occasionally was even physically abusive, slapping, hitting, and kicking his sister.

Their parent's reaction to all this was, "Oh, Joe, I wish you'd stop that," or, "Oh, all kids fight. They'll grow out of it," and occasionally, "All brothers and sisters squabble; we just let them work it out themselves."

The only trouble with "letting them work it out themselves" (which amounted to letting them *fight* it out) was the effect it was having on Karen. In Karen's eyes she was a bad person, worthless, not valuable to her parents because they didn't care enough to stop her brother from hurting her and making her life miserable. As a consequence she grew up with a totally negative self-image. This is common to all abused and battered people, the more so when the batterer is a person who is supposed to love them or, as in Karen's situation, when a person who is supposed to love them won't stop the abuse.

Of course, people who knew them felt there was something wrong behind her parents' attitude. They did not want a girl when Karen was born, and even after Joe came along they were not happy with Karen because she was big and husky and not the delicate little china doll they had pictured themselves as having. Their favoritism for Joe was obvious.

Karen never married, and although she is extremely smart she has had little career success. Her early years have left her with an insecurity, a low opinion of herself and her ability, and also a rage that explodes at the worst times and often toward people who have done nothing to deserve it.

Christie's mother is a neurotic, negative woman, the sort who gives every cloud a pitch-black lining. Her husband (understandably, according to many people) left her for another woman, and she is taking out her anger at him and at the world on her two teenage children.

According to her, Christie is "clumsy, dumb, and stupid." "According to my mother," Christie says sadly, "I have never done one thing right in my whole life."

Christie's brother, Ron, is obviously very smart, so Mother's jabs don't include "dumb." He is, according to her, "Ugly. You are the homeliest thing I've ever had the misfortune to see."

Both children have lived with this for years. Not a day goes by without both of them feeling the lash of her tongue. Of course, the mother has a serious emotional problem. The real tragedy is that she is passing it along to her son and daughter, giving them a view of themselves as bad and worthless people, a view that is totally warped and also totally incorrect.

Josh's parents are loving and not neurotic. But they are undemonstrative people and members of a rigorous religion that teaches, "Spare the rod and spoil the child."

Josh's parents do spare the rod; he has had only a few spankings in his life. But they are afraid of spoiling him (and their other children). To them, compliments and praise are "spoiling." Not praising him for something he has done will, they think, "spur him to do still better."

So while Josh doesn't get negative feedback from his parents, he gets very little positive reaction either. He works hard on the family farm but seldom gets so much as "You did a good job" from his father or mother. Privileges, such as extra spending money now and then or use of the family car, also come under the category of "spoiling," and Josh gets few of them.

Josh is certainly not spoiled, but he has very low self-esteem. Since nothing he does seems good enough to earn praise from his parents or any sort of reward but a grunt, he sees everything he does—and himself—as inferior and unworthy. His self-image is not actually bad, like the other teens mentioned, just negative and limited.

Imagine a youngster who has had to live in the shadow of a brother or sister. "Why can't *you* make as good grades as Jimmy?" "Too bad you didn't make the team, especially since your brother was All-Conference quarterback." "This is our daughter, Susan, who was Homecoming Queen, Rose Princess at the Summer Festival, and runner-up in Junior Miss—and this is our other daughter, Linda." Such a youngster would need the hide of a rhinoceros and an inner makeup mainly of steel not to see himself or herself as second-rate, second-best, just not good enough.

The sad thing in such situations is that young people often don't realize that their problems are coming from an outside source. They think they feel inferior because they *are* inferior. They never guess that someone else—often without intending to do it—has programmed them into a poor self-image.

Contrary to the beliefs of people like Josh's parents, absence of spoiling, praise, or rewards will not "spur you on." It is against basic human nature for us to keep struggling when we aren't gaining anything by it. When we don't gain anything, we begin to see ourselves as not worth anything.

Overcoming such a handicap can take tremendous effort. Many people never manage it.

What if the victim of such "programming" is you? Often people don't realize they are in exactly this spot.

Finding a sympathetic adult to talk to can help a great deal. The problem is, however, that many adults don't recognize, "I feel like I can't ever do anything right!" as a painful cry for help. Too often the response is, "Don't be silly. Of course you do!" Many young people don't seek outside help because they are sure that other adults will side with their parents (or whoever the guilty party is) and they'll get another put-down they neither want nor need.

Consider discussing things with a school counselor. Don't shy off because you can't put your finger on a specific problem. "I just don't feel good about myself. I feel like I can't do anything right, like there's nothing good about me. I can't turn around without getting my head bitten off. I feel like a real failure," is a perfectly good reason to try to get help.

Not all counselor-patient personalities blend well, however. If you feel the counselor isn't taking you seriously or isn't doing much for you, seek someone else. A favorite teacher, your minister, perhaps your youth activities director at church might help. A note of warning: Some ministers are wonderful with people with problems, but some make things worse. If yours is the hellfire and brimstone, rigid and condemning type, you'd probably be better off steering clear. Perhaps a friend who goes to another church or synagogue can recommend a minister, rabbi, or counselor to consult.

The most important thing, however, is to get and keep a clear view of yourself as you really are. According to her mother, Christie is "dumb and stupid." Christie doesn't stop to think that she makes very good grades and has won honors and awards in several fields. She only sees the things she does poorly.

So don't make Christie's mistake. Whenever you have done something well, achieved a great grade, performed outstandingly at something, solved a real problem, keep a written record of it. Get a little notebook (we are great at recommending things written in "little notebooks," aren't we?) and on each page write something good about yourself. Once again, it's as well not to let anyone else in on this. "Bragging on yourself?" is likely to be the response from the negative-trip person in your life. Hide your little book, and once or twice a day get it out and look at it. Our memories play tricks on us, but if you have there, written down in black and white, a record of the good and positive things about yourself, the things you can really do, it can help to counterbalance the negative input.

Like most efforts to make a change in ourselves, nothing works if done only now and then. This must be done over and over again. Two or three days isn't going to put much of a dent in mind games that may have been going on for years.

Work to see the good in yourself. Don't go over and over problems or put-downs or real failures. Think of solutions and then carry them out. We believe you can reprogram your way of thinking.

As much as you can, stay away from negative people and people who, even indirectly, put you down. Think positive.

Sorry to sound as if we write slogans for a poster company. These things do sound trite and cliched—but they also work if you work at making them work.

Not long ago we saw a young man wearing a T-shirt that proclaimed, "Life is a bitch and then you die." Maybe he thought it was cute. We think anyone would be better off spending the afternoon with someone who had a raging case of the plague. That would be our choice, anyway. Plague can make you afraid you are going to die. An outlook on life like that can make you afraid you won't.

CHAPTER XVII

More Than a "Touch" of Class

Mention manners or a lecture on manners to a group of teens and you get howls, groans, and corny imitations of 1917 society ladies sipping tea with lifted pinkies. So let's not use the word manners. Let's use another word that means pretty much the same thing: manners with a high gloss on them. Class.

This whole book has been about dressing and looking as if you have a lot of class. But class is not, at the bottom line, something determined by the way you dress, your looks, or your money. In fact, as you know yourself if you just look around, the world is full of people who have great looks and great bucks and all the class of a Skid Row resident. If you look great and your wardrobe could start a boutique in business and you still fit that last category, the contrast is going to make everything wrong more noticeable: If you are basically a clod, it jumps out and hits people in the face.

What is class, anyway?

It's basically the golden rule: treating people as you would want to be treated. It's grace under fire, being at your best under pressure. The person with class isn't a wimp or a doormat; class means treating *yourself* well, too. There are plenty of times—especially when you are a teen—when your best move is to stand up firmly for your own rights and to sing your own praises. But there has to be a basic concern for the rights and feelings of others as well.

Here are some examples of no-class behavior. Do you recognize yourself anywhere?

• Something has happened to your best friend that embarrassed him or her a great deal, but it does make a great story. Telling the story will win you a lot of attention and a lot of laughs, although it will hurt your friend. You go on and tell the story. What the heck? It wasn't really that bad, and he or she will get over it.

• You go to a fancy restaurant with candles on the table in cute little holders that would look great in your room. "They expect people to do this, they even plan it into the budget. Besides, they charge you plenty here," you say, as you blow out the candle, wait for the holder to cool, and then slip it into a pocket.

• Your room looks as if you have been keeping a tornado for a pet, but you are "too busy" listening to music, watching TV, playing video games, or just hanging out to clean it up.

• Christmas is coming and you think, "Why bother spending the extra money?" so you wrap up for someone else the bottle of cologne your Great Aunt Matilda gave you last year—the bottle that, when you open it, the houseplant nearest you dies, your cat flees with hair on end, and flies fall off the ceiling dead from the fumes.

• You draw names in a club or your home room and are told there's a limit, $3 or $5 or whatever. Instead of taking a little time to hunt a gift, you get a "gag" gift (most of them make you want to) from the "joke shop."

(If you don't care enough to spend a little time and effort on getting a gift, we'd say don't bother to get anything. Sleazy gifts are sleazy gifts. They're an insult, and most people would rather get nothing.)

• You receive a nice gift, and when asked if you have written a thank-you note, you say, "No, I didn't get around to it. Anyway, nobody does that any more. They know I like what I got." A call to say "Thank you" is the very least gesture you can make. A note of thanks is what the person with class sends.

Total silence is flat rude; we personally have a strong impulse to take back whatever it was we gave.

• You're invited to a party on which friends have spent a lot of time and money to make a really special occasion. You say, "I'm too tired to change. Anyway, nobody dresses up anymore," and you turn up in clothes more appropriate for changing the oil in the car. The dress may well be casual, but your not bothering to find out and clumping in looking like a slob is rude.

(Are you beginning to see why most people want to put a kid who fits this category over their knee? How do *you* like it when you are on the receiving end of such thoughtless, selfish behavior?)

• You go to a friend's house and walk in right in the middle of a big family fight. Before long you've given a dozen people a detailed account of every scream and yell.

• You're on a diet, so you say, "I'll skip the popcorn at the movie" or "I'm broke, I'll just watch you guys eat" when everyone else is chipping in for pizza. You don't pay, but somehow you manage to wind up eating as much as everyone else.

• You are always borrowing something—money, clothes, tapes, school supplies, whatever. Sure, anyone can be caught short now and then, but it's Slobsville to sit back and expect your friends to keep you supplied.

We could go on and on, but we won't. Chances are you don't notice this behavior so much in other people your age. You are, after all, still working at the process of becoming people who get along in an adult world. There are even some of you (not specifically *you*, but teens in general) who think it is macho or cool—or whatever the current word is—not to have manners, to act like an obnoxious slob. You walk in, take a soft drink out of someone else's hand and gulp it down, and expect people to admire you. Maybe some rather dim specimens do. But we are now talking—and have been all along—about the adult world.

Adults call the shots. And bad manners in young people make them stand out like an Angus cow in a snowbank. In the adult world, lack of class is going to hurt you—don't ever doubt it.

And class, real class, can do more for your image than a mink coat.

CHAPTER XVIII

Eating and Images

Kristy is all excited. She's fifteen and a sophomore, and her grandmother has just promised that if Kristy wants to pledge a sorority when she goes to college, grandma will foot the bill. Kristy has high dreams and good enough grades and ambitions to interest a sorority. She has in mind the sorority her best friend's sister pledged. Through sorority activities the sister got a job in TV production and lives in New York with her millionaire husband. "That's what I'm going for!" Kristy announces.

Kristy has a lot going for her—and one big thing going against her. As she talks about the sorority now, her mouth is full and she isn't bothering to close it when she chews. People sitting at the table behind her can hear Kristy eating. Some of her lunch is on her chin and some of it on her T-shirt. The unfortunate fact is that Kristy's table manners would be more at home in a barn. And that's going to hurt.

Did we hear some of you say, "That's a crock!" We probably did. Unfortunately, people who believe that have to learn the hard way that it isn't. Employees have missed out on promotions, high school seniors have lost bids to go to military academy, coveted fraternity and sorority bids or club memberships have gone by, medical students have missed out on the residency program they wanted, all because of poor table manners.

A high school principal tells about the time when several movie stars visited his school, which had been used in the filming of a major made-for-TV movie. "They came to lunch, and of course there was cut-throat rivalry to see who would sit at the head table with us. I was for going on scholastic and sports honors, but the home economics teacher said I'd better audition table manners before I made any choices, if I didn't want to be awfully embarrassed. Was she ever right! Out of the twenty kids who were my first choices, only two had the least idea how to behave in such a situation."

He was silent for a moment. "It's sad, when you come to think of it. Parents don't teach kids how to behave anymore, it seems. Families don't eat together as they used to. They eat in front of the TV, or snack in shifts. There's no emphasis on manners. It's hard to blame the kids if they haven't been brought up with manners. It's not their fault, but they are the ones who suffer."

The idea that manners don't matter is a leftover from the hippie way of thinking. In that time, the 1960s and early '70s, good manners were not only not important, they were faintly suspect. To act halfway civilized at meals could get you branded with that horrible label "Establishment."

Well, to quote a song title of that era, the times they are a-changing. The Greek system is making a strong comeback after the beating it took in those days. High school and college standards are getting tougher, not looser. Drug users and heavy drinkers are more likely to be considered "roaches" (which certainly doesn't mean what it did then!) than cool or neat. "Space cadet" is a slam.

The hippie rebels are corporate executives now, and do they shovel and cram food into their mouths, belch, sprawl on elbows on the table? Of course not! Furthermore—and most of them will be honest about it—when it comes to promoting younger people they usually have lunch with the candidate before making a decision. Believe us, his or her manners will play a big role in the decision.

As one chairman of the board put it, "A lot of company

business is done over lunch or dinner tables. You don't consider hiring or promoting people who will make your company look bad. And poor manners make it look bad.''

If you haven't learned at home, how do you acquire the polish for the image that will help you get what you want in life? Unfortunately, that can be difficult. But you learn by imitation. Go to lunch at a restaurant popular with the people who do what you think you'd like to do, and watch them. (Lunch is usually affordable, even on an allowance.) Watch them. Take notes. Actual notes help more than just mental jottings. Begin, yourself, to imitate.

We also recommend a good book on etiquette. If that conjures up visions of stiff little old ladies in white gloves and frumpy hats, well, etiquette books have been like that in the past, but few are any more. We especially recommend *Miss Manners' Guide to Excruciatingly Correct Behavior*. It is not only one of the best, most practical, and contemporary books we have seen on the subject, it is also hilarious; it's worth reading just for entertainment as well as the smarts it contains.

There's more to table manners—or maybe we should say food manners—than using the right fork, however, and in this area teens are about the worst offenders.

Recently one of the authors made an enormous tossed salad while an assortment of teenage nieces and nephews hovered in the background supplying a Greek chorus of "What's *that?*" (There was an overwhelming urge on the part of the author to upend the bowl over certain heads.)

One nephew finally was brave enough to give a new item a try. That had the effect of making the others shut up and also venture a nibble or two. They were astonished to find that kiwi bore no resemblance to hemlock, they could eat a mushroom and survive, and raw zucchini was actually good.

Being a picky eater, turning up your nose at something before you so much as taste it, is both childish and hickish. It makes a very poor impression when you approach a new type of food as though you were sure it was laced with arsenic. Don't get us wrong: You are certainly entitled not to like something. Some people would sell the gold filling in their teeth to buy fresh asparagus; one of the authors would rather chew on the kind of old carpet that should be burned five miles outside the city limits. But she at least has *tried* asparagus. Her preference is based on knowledge, not "Ick, that looks terrible!"

If you know you don't like something—such as liver or brussels sprouts, or whatever—don't eat it, but also keep quiet about it. Nobody wants to hear a sermon on the time that tuna casserole made you sick or how you just can't stand avocados. Act halfway mature about it. Don't eat it, but don't make a big production out of it. This is especially true if you are at someone else's house. To talk about how you hate a dish being served may make the hostess want to heat it to the boiling point and pour it down the back of your neck.

One hostess, commenting angrily on an adult who painstakingly went through a salad taking out onions and black olives, said furiously, "He acted as if he were looking for *bugs*, peering at every bite. There'll be a strong cold snap before he gets invited here again!"

Even if you don't like it, eat it with as much grace as possible. It won't kill you, and life isn't all grand opera, you know. If choking down a bite or two of avocado, liver, or whatever is the worst thing that ever happens to you in this life, you'll have made it through pretty well.

CHAPTER XIX

"Turn That #%&#–#!! Radio Down!"*

At this writing, one of the most outstanding fads in your age group (and younger), aside from anything Michael Jackson, is the suitcase-sized radio, usually carried on the shoulder and turned to a volume that would shatter glass and make mortar crumble between bricks.

According to a psychologist friend, the purpose of these radios is not to listen to the music; much of the time the volume is so high that the music is an indistinguishable blur of sound. The purpose is to keep people at arm's length and—like the songs of birds—to stake out one's own territory. Occasionally they are used for simple aggression: "It's a free country. If you don't like my music this loud, go somewhere else. I gotta right to listen to what I want!" A radio tuned to ear-shattering volume is like the old chip on the shoulder: The owner is daring anyone to do something about it.

We have promised to stick strictly to images, and we will. The giant portable radio has two image elements, and both are strongly negative.

The slang term for it is "ghetto blaster," and that's the image it gives the carrier. It doesn't matter if you drive up in a Rolls Silver Ghost, the image persists.

The other image aspect is much more subtle. It's one of those odd cases in which the human brain knows instinctively what it takes scientists years to learn, document, and prove.

The image that goes with music played at high volume is "dumb." "That person is short on smarts upstairs." A university freshman dorm counselor told us, "When we have to tell someone several times to turn down the radio or stereo, that they are bothering other people, I find myself saying 'That one won't last more than a semester.' It's true more often than not. When someone says 'I can't study without the radio on,' I have found that most of the time—not always, but most of the time—that person isn't a good student, can't hack it at the college level. In my experience, the scholarship-level students want it quiet."

Recently experts have found that babies and young children brought up in households where the radio or TV was kept at blast volume for long periods of time were far behind other kids in development. "It's just too loud for them to learn," one doctor said. "They are less active mentally, often far behind the learning level where they should be. Often they are not active physically. It's almost as if the noise has hammered them into submission. We've seen a few cases where a child has been judged to be retarded until it got into a quiet environment, and then the brain began to wake up."

So if you want to blast the plaster off the ceiling, kill the houseplants, and send the family cat or dog into shellshock with high volume at home, that's between you and your family. In public the image it will get you from adults and from more of your peers than you realize is "dim, really *dim*."

CHAPTER XX

"I'm Sorry, So Sorry. . ."

That was the title of a country and western song popular a few years back and still resurrected now and again. Let's consider "I'm sorry" and the image teens have.

The old "advice to teens" book we mentioned earlier often had a section on apologizing. It was stressed that apologizing was an art and a grace and that being able to do it was desirable, especially for girls.

Certainly if you are overwhelmingly in the wrong about something, being able to say you are sorry can smooth things over. People who say, "I just can't apologize, no matter what," are in effect saying, "I am not going to admit I an wrong even if you threaten me!" and that's certainly a negative attitude.

But the fact is that for many people—girls and women much more than males—"I'm sorry" has become a phrase they tack onto conversations, scatter through sentences, and often use without having the least idea they are doing it or of the impression it is creating.

"I'm sorry, I didn't hear what you said."

"I'm sorry you didn't get the part in the play you tried out for."

"I'm sorry, did you want that last piece of candy I ate?"

"I'm sorry" implies that you are somehow to blame, that what happened was your fault. In any of the above cases, was it really? Probably not. The person speaking has as much obligation to make himself or herself clear as the listener does to understand what is being said. Unless the person speaking got the part, he or she isn't responsible for the other person's not getting it. Unless the person who ate the candy flattened the other one in a mad dash for the bowl, he doesn't owe the slowpoke an apology.

A therapist friend says, "Every time you say 'I'm sorry' when it really isn't warranted or what happened wasn't your fault, you seem to shrink. 'I'm sorry, I'm sorry, I'm sorry'. . .until you are a shriveled up nothing, still apologizing, huddled in a corner."

He may have been exaggerating for the sake of making a point, and "I'm sorry" may not always register on the conscious brain (unlike "You know"), but the argument is basically true. An unwarranted apology does register subconsciously, and it's a powerfully negative image element.

Synonyms for sorry are mean, vile, poor, second-rate, beggarly, shabby, low-class, worthless. How often have you tacked that definition onto yourself and not even realized it? Probably more often than you think.

The people who say, "I just can't apologize" usually seem proud of it, as though it were an admirable trait. It isn't, of course, and it's just as negative as too much "I'm sorry."

The trick is to hit the right blend.

Of course we all goof, we all make mistakes, and we all do things to be sorry about. We're all human, in other words. The refusal to say, "I did this and I know it was wrong. I apologize and will take the blame" was the basic element that toppled the Nixon presidency.

When you are in the wrong about something, when something is your fault, have the guts to admit it and say, "Look, I really messed up and I apologize. Let me get the problem straight, okay?"

One good apology is all you owe. If you keep apologizing for something one of two thing is happening. Either you are into the "I'm sorry - I'm sorry - I'm sorry" syndrome, in which case you need to start breaking out; or the other person or people are putting a *"You're* sorry" guilt and blame trip on you, in which case you need to recognize the problem and get out from under their loading it on you.

"I apologize" is all you need to say. Comb "I'm sorry" out of your vocabulary, just as you do (or we hope are trying to) "You know" and "Huh?"

You may be in the wrong sometimes. We all are. But that doesn't mean that you fit the dictionary definition of "sorry," so don't go around tacking that image on yourself.

CHAPTER XXI

"You Wanna Make Something of It?"

A teacher friend confessed that she couldn't stand a boy in her class; in fact, her aversion was so strong that she finally asked the principal to transfer him. That was done, although the boy protested strongly: He liked the teacher, and he didn't want to go into a much rougher class with a teacher who handed out three times as much homework.

"The first day that little beast walked in the door I bristled," she recalled, "and no matter how I tried to talk myself out of it, I couldn't even stand him, much less like him. I despised him, and I knew I could never be fair." (At least she was honest enough to admit her feelings and not spend the year taking them out on the student.)

What caused such a strong reaction?

The first day of class the boy had worn a T-shirt with a printed message: "Help stamp out rape! Say yes."

He thought it was funny, and so did some of his friends. (There *are* insensitive clods like that in the world.) But the teacher had been raped when she was eleven years old, by a brutal creature who was later convicted of a double murder. It was a nightmare for her that, years later, she had not completely got over.

And now here was this unspeakable creep in the front row saying she should have gone along with that skin-crawling goon all those years ago!

Granted, that reaction isn't likely to happen, but if the boy had thought about it, he wasn't saying anything admirable about himself with the shirt and it wasn't going to have a good

effect on most people he met. But he didn't think—and he suffered the consequences. (Life has a way of handing out consequences to people who don't think, you know.)

T-shirts are bumper stickers for humans, and unfortunately,
a lot of kids don't stop and look at the message they are
screaming at the world.

Put-downs, proclaiming the glory of booze and dope, ethnic
slurs—the range of T-shirt messages is amazing. Some are funny, most are trite and overdone, a few are outright offensive.

Before you go to school in a shirt with a message, use your
head. Are there people it might hurt? Make angry? Offend?
You should be smart enough to know.

If you insist on wearing a shirt that proclaims how much
beer you can drink, or that life is better if you stay high, or that
people should avoid hangovers by staying drunk, at least have
the guts to live with the consequences.

We recall a young man just out of high school who appeared
at work on his first day wearing a T-shirt that was genuinely
obscene. Quite naturally, his supervisor hit the roof and
ordered him to change it. He changed, sullenly, but he and the
supervisor were off on the wrong foot from the beginning.
Three days later he wore a shirt proclaiming, in graphic terms,
what a great lover he was, and the next day his shirt said he
couldn't decide which he liked better, whiskey or dope.

To no one's surprise, the young man didn't last two weeks,
and when he was fired he moaned, whined, and even tried to
file a lawsuit alleging discrimination.

The term "chip on the shoulder" came from an era, perhaps
the time of Tom Sawyer, when a bully or someone itching for a
fight would put a chip of wood on a shoulder and dare anyone
to knock it off.

Offensive T-shirts aren't that openly honest. They have their stated message and their hidden message: "This is the way I feel—wanna make something of it?"

You started it; don't snivel and whine if someone takes you up on the challenge.

CHAPTER XXII

The Image That You Want for You

Okay, so what does all this mean *you* need to do, to create the best image you want for where you want to go and what you want to do in life?

It helps if you know exactly what you do want.

You may not know. Many students are nearly through college before they know what they really want to do. But chances are good that you at least know the general type of career you want, the general area of work you'd most like to do. For example, if you have lived most of your life in the country, enjoy outdoor activities, and the thought of a nine-to-five office job sounds about as appealing as a twenty-year prison term, it isn't likely that you'll gravitate toward being a stockbroker, doctor, or lawyer, but rather to a career as a ranch manager, bloodstock agent, or large-animal veterinarian.

If you turn to the business section and the stock market quotations before you do the sports or even the front page, three-piece suits and tailored wools almost certainly loom in your future.

When you think you have a general area in mind, study role models: people who are successful at what you want to do. How do they dress? How do they act and react around other people? We are not saying you should slavishly copy everything these people do, but rather use them as a general guide for your own clothes and look. If banking is the field that fascinates you, you'll learn one style of dress and manner that seems common to successful people in that field. If you would like nothing better than to manage a farm for running quarter horses, you'll find that people at the top of the success ladder go almost everywhere in jeans, a tailored shirt, and boots.

Maybe you haven't homed in that much on what you want, but you'd still like to create the best image possible.

Why not? It isn't spineless or wimpish or losing your own identity; it's giving yourself all the advantages.

The top-drawer look is almost always your best bet. (We can't think of a situation where it isn't.) Don't go out on a limb, or spend money you don't have, or nag your parents about it. You can probably do a lot to recreate an image without spending a cent. Some improvements even save money, like saying let lightning flatten you if you ever chew another piece of gum, or swearing to quit smoking now (while it's a whole lot easier than it will be farther down the road).

Make a game of changing your image. Make specific plans and write them down: "My goal this month is to lose fifteen pounds and have my hair restyled." Then write out the ways you are going to reach that goal. As for losing the weight, that might just take leaving out the candy bars between classes. Substitute an apple or, better yet, celery stalks (celery has a natural ingredient that slightly suppresses the appetite). Celery may not taste as good as candy, but even better than candy is seeing your outline shrink, feeling your clothes fit better, seeing them look better, feeling better about yourself.

Make a month's plan, and make what you want to do reasonable and relatively easy. Don't go overboard.

Plan rewards for yourself along the way. (We *don't* mean reward yourself for the loss of three pounds by consuming a chocolate soda. So many people do that and in the long run never accomplish anything at all.)

One young friend has a good system of rewards. Every time she doesn't give in and buy something fattening or that might make her face break out, she puts the money into a small bank.

At the end of the month she takes whatever is in the bank and buys herself something nice with it. She's a winner all the way around—no overweight, no zits, and money spent on a wardrobe that is beginning to be fabulous.

We recommend another way, too. Get a notebook, one small enough to hide away if you have a nosy family. In the front paste a picture of someone you like and think you might have a chance to look like. Then set goals for yourself, projects that will take time—like losing weight, adding some muscle. Put down your goal on the second page and on the third page the weight you are now, or the state of the problem you want to correct, such as a poor complexion or a scruffy and unflattering wardrobe.

Next make a page for things that should require less effort, such as getting "Yeah" and "Huh?" out of your vocabulary. Now make a page for each improvement, and across the top put what it is going to take to make changes and reach your goal. Be specific.

Measure your progress. One good way with weight loss is to write down your present weight, then weigh every week and note the decrease.

At the end of each week sit down and see how well you have done. If you are happy with your success, give yourself a reward. Dress up and have an afternoon of window shopping in the plushest shopping center around. (We promise you'll learn a lot, and that goes for boys as well as girls.) Treat yourself to a horseback ride. Spend some of the money you've saved on video games. Go to a museum that has something special. Go to a laser rock show.

If some of these things are a little different from your usual activities, what's wrong with beginning to break away from the "every teenager out of the same cookie cutter" image? Nothing at all. You'll be a more interesting person for it.

CHAPTER XXIII

Shopping Smarts (for Boys as Well as Girls)

If you are thinking about clothes that upgrade your image and you don't have all kinds of cash to spend, do a little planning about the money you will spend for what you want.

Be wary of "the" thing *everyone* feels they must have right now. Unfortunately, within three or four months it will be totally dated and you won't want to be seen in it. That's probably the area of most waste with people your age.

Here are some ideas to help make your money go farther and do more for you.

Consider getting haircuts and manicures at a beauty college. (They do men's and boys' hair, too.) Students will be working on you, but they are supervised by instructors and you can be sure of getting the latest style, often before you can get it at a regular salon, and for about one-fourth the price you'd pay otherwise.

Of course, there's no guarantee you'll be happy with the result; there's no guarantee you'll be thrilled with the result in the highest-priced place in town. One of the authors recently had a fairly high-dollar haircut that was a disaster, and her first reaction on seeing it in the mirror was, "Did anybody get the number of that Indian? I could shoot her, and no all-female jury on earth would convict me!" The disaster stayed disastrous for about two weeks and then looked quite good. That's one thing about hair and nails: Whatever you have done to them isn't plastic surgery. It'll always grow out.

Of course, if you don't trust the cut-rate emporium or the student your own age, have the high-style shop cut your hair.

Get someone to take pictures of you from all sides, and *then* go to the reasonably priced shop and tell them you want your hair done just as it is in the picture.

When you have the image you are reaching for pretty well in mind, start going to the stores that sell top-of-the-line clothes for that look. Notice we didn't say "go shopping" at those stores. At first you should just be looking. Study the cut of the clothes, the material, the lines, the little details. It's amazing the difference details can make. One author had a home economics class take part in an experiment using a blazer that had originally cost $50. Three successive sets of buttons were put on it, and it was shown to three different groups of college home economics students. With the cheapest possible dull plastic buttons, the average price guessed for the blazer was $20. When expensive, dyed mother-of-pearl buttons were sewed on, the estimated cost was $85. When gold-plated monogrammed buttons were added, the guessed cost was about $125. Details like that have tremendous clout, and often they are things you can do yourself to clothes you already have or clothes you buy. And even boys should be able to sew on buttons!

Study the people who shop in these stores—their grooming, makeup, hair style, even the way they talk. Before long you will begin to pick up many of the little things that make up the image of the world you want.

And this isn't phony, any more than going to high school or college is "phony." The end result of it all is to get you where you want to go in life, isn't it?

Spend the most on clothes from these stores or that most nearly resemble clothes from these stores. They are most likely to look well now and for a long time to come.

Check "outlet" stores in your area. Sometimes they sell sleazy junk, but often you can find excellent buys. After all, a cashmere sweater is a cashmere sweater, whether it sells in the high-priced store for $140 or with the label cut out in the outlet store for $50.

Be careful of fad items. Sure, they are fun and part of your identity as a teen and a member of "your" group at school, but they can also gobble up a lot of money and have the life span of a May fly. Fad items generally follow a definite price trend. At first and for a very short time they are expensive, because they are hot items—everybody wants one right now. Then the price breaks and thereafter drops like a rock, because store buyers know the item's a fad and before long they couldn't pay someone to take it.

If everything you wear has some fad element or fad look, you *are* making a statement by what you wear. The statement says, "I'm not sure who I am; I don't even have an identity right now, so I just wear the latest thing in style." Fad clothes sometimes seem to be walking around without a real person inside them.

Before you pay much, take a long look at the garment and ask yourself how likely it is to stay in style. Michael Jackson jackets are hot right now, but they are a version of a style that has been around for years and that looks well on most people; they're a fad but likely to be in fashion for a long time. On the other hand, cropped pants are new and different and you see them everywhere, but they are basically ugly and not very flattering. They make your feet look enormous and give even the graceful a clumsy, ducklike walk. We could be wrong, of course. (Wrong! Us!?!) But we don't think this style will be around long. Some years back, during the heyday of Jackie Kennedy as First Lady, coats had sleeves that stopped just a little past the elbow. They could look elegant, but basically a coat with half a sleeve is a pretty silly idea, and that style had a short life span.

Don't pay high prices for fad or "high style" items. Discount stores, "dime" stores, little "budget" shops are the places to go for those things. Save better boutique and department store money for classic clothes you know will be working for your image and your goals a year or two or three from now.

CHAPTER XXIV

The Bottom Line

Do you see "image" in a different light now than you did when you started this book? We hope so. Image is a lot of things, but it isn't or shouldn't be, the kind of phony, plastic facade people tend to think of. When your image is right, not only do people give you a chance to show your brains and abilities, but you find you have more brains and abilities to show. Your image gives you the confidence to do and to be your best. The self-fulfilling prophecy, the energy loop.

Can you get by on a totally phony image? Movie and recording stars obviously have done so; witness some of the books written about them and what they are really like. Good grief, any person seeing them in their true light and meeting them face to face would run a mile. Of course, few of their fans or following ever meet them face to face.

You, on the other hand, do have to deal one-on-one with the people in your life. You can get along for a while with a phony image, but only for a while. Then the image starts to backfire, and it can really hurt you. If your image promises something that you don't deliver, that confuses people and they feel negatively toward you. They may not understand exactly why they feel that way, but the fact remains that they do. If you come across as a potentially excellent employee and then spend half the day on the phone and the other half making blunders with your mind obviously elsewhere, people will be not only annoyed at the goofs but angry at you, as if you had in some way lied to them.

A good image isn't "how to succeed in business without really trying." It's the red carpet to get you to the place where you can really try.

So go for it, get there, do your best. It is, after all, *your* life, and our lives tend to be pretty much what WE make of them.

Good luck to you, in everything you want that is fun and good and really worthwhile!